FORGIVING HITLER

the KATHY DIOSY story

as told by

KEL RICHARDS

Foreword by

PHILLIP D. JENSEN

MATTHIAS MEDIA

Forgiving Hitler
© Beacon Communications, 2002
originally published in Australia by Matthias Media, Sydney

Published in the United Kingdom by:
The Good Book Company
Tel: 0845 225 0880
Fax: 0845 225 0990
email: admin@thegoodbook.co.uk
www.thegoodbook.co.uk

ISBN 1 876326 49 2

Cover design and typesetting by Joy Lankshear Design Pty Ltd.

Printed in the UK by Bookmarque.

COVER PHOTO: *The crowd of spectators at the 1936 Olympic Games in Berlin raises their hands in the Nazi salute in tribute to the Führer's arrival at the stadium.* AUSTRALIAN PICTURE LIBRARY.

DEDICATED TO
MY GRANDCHILDREN
Forgive, but don't forget...

A NOTE ABOUT NAMES

At birth she was given the
name "Katalin Eva Kalafoni".
As a young woman she was
known as "Kitty".
Her married surname is Diosy,
and to most of her friends today
she is "Kathy".
In the interests of historical accu-
racy, the name "Kitty Kalafoni"
is used in this book.

FOREWORD

YOU HAVE IN YOUR HANDS a most extraordinary story: the title itself warns you of its extraordinary character. *Forgiving Hitler* is about as obscene a title as one could imagine for a book.

Then again Kathy Diosy is a most extraordinary person—as you will come to discover. This book is not a complete biography of Kathy's life. It does not tell you all the details of her past. It does not detail all the dreadful things that were done to her or that she has done. It doesn't linger over the sordid details of an evil world for the entertainment of vulgar or violent minds. It is true that forgiveness is found in facing, not denying, reality. But it is also true that forgiveness is neither found nor expressed in the endless rehearsal of the details of offence. And crucially, real forgiveness involves the victim's release from victimology.

Forgiveness is important in whatever form it takes or level at which it operates. Forgiveness is about relationships, about improving relationships, about restoring relationships. This alone makes it important. In our litigious culture and in our age of war, hostility and divorce, learning how to mend and repair relationships must be important.

Forgiveness often helps the injured party as much if not more than the offender. It removes from the injured the sense of rage and bitterness, the sense of outraged injustice, the disappointment in life that colours everything else. It also removes from us that self-deception that we are all prone to: that the offender is the only person who has done something wrong in life and that I, as the perfectly innocent sufferer, have the right to judge others. This is to play God.

Forgiveness is also very difficult to achieve. Injustice is a reality not just a feeling—just as evil is a reality not just an opinion. It is a minor thing to forgive a minor inconvenience. But to forgive the betrayal of a hateful abuser of your trust—that is a pain almost unbearable. It feels like being the victim twice over and then some.

Kathy's journey in life was one shared by the countless millions who suffered the horrors of Hitler's rampage. She was one of that generation of survivors that we must listen to. We must hear the horror of the reality of evil and never be satisfied with the trite removal of 'iniquity' and 'sin' from our vocabulary by the spin doctors of ethical relativism. But we must also hear the story of how the survivors reconstructed their lives. We must hear the story of finding forgiveness.

When you have finished reading this book, I am sure that you will be thankful that she has shared it with us, and thankful for the skill of Kel Richards in presenting Kathy's painful and difficult story so clearly and sensitively. I am also thankful to God, that he has dealt so kindly with my friend and sister, and given me the privilege of knowing such an extraordinary woman.

Phillip D. Jensen

DESCENDANTS OF JACOB KALAFONI AND JULIANNA ROTH

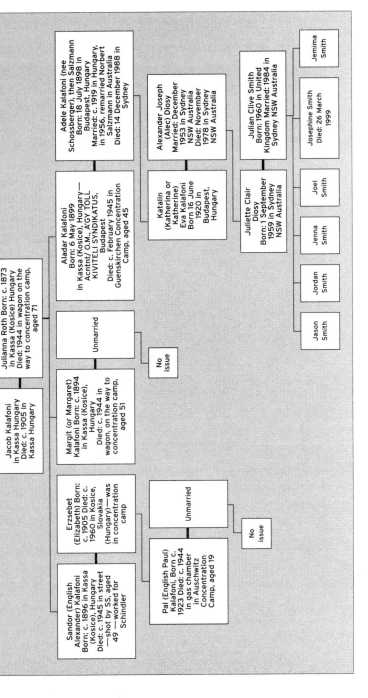

Kathy Diosy (1939)

I

AUSTRIAN PRESIDENT Willhelm Miklas was listening to a furious Adolf Hitler shouting down the phone line. Unless Austria submitted to all the demands being made within the hour, German troops would march across the border. It was six thirty in the evening, and the day had been a long and difficult one for Miklas.

'Within the hour,' repeated Hitler. 'That is my last word.'

'Once more, I refuse, Herr Hitler,' replied Miklas. 'Austria alone determines who is to be the head of the Austrian government.'

'You have sealed your own fate,' said the German dictator as he hung up.

The calendar on Miklas's desk read 11 March, 1938. With a hand that trembled slightly, more in anger than fear, he drew a circle around that date—a date, he was certain, Austrian school children would be learning about in history lessons for many decades to come.

At dawn that morning the Germans had closed the German-Austrian border. For over a year Hitler, the Nazi Chancellor of Germany, had been demanding that neighbouring Austria surrender its sovereignty and self-government, and submit to German rule. On this Friday in March those demands were reaching their tense climax.

During the afternoon Hitler had bombarded the Austrian Chancellor, Kurt von Schuschnigg, with aggressive phone calls demanding his resignation. Hitler insisted that an Austrian Nazi leader, Dr Arthur Seyss-Inquart, be appointed as Chancellor in Schuschnigg's place.

As the afternoon dragged on, Schuschnigg gave in to the

pressure and resigned. However, as President of Austria, Willhelm Miklas, refused to appoint Hitler's nominee as his replacement.

Meanwhile, Nazi headquarters in Germany was in contact with the Austrian Nazi party. Phone calls quickly rounded up the fanatically dedicated members of the Austrian party, and they were told to take to the streets demanding complete surrender to Hitler and integration into Germany.

'Within the hour,' Hitler had said. 'That is my last word.'

2

'WHAT DRESS SHOULD I wear tonight?' asked Kitty Kalafoni, turning to the Slovakian girl with whom she shared the room.

'The pink one, perhaps? You know, with the pearl buttons.'

'I'm saving that,' said Kitty, 'for the opera.'

'Well, what about that light blue one with the little silver squares in it?'

'I wore that last week.'

'If you don't want it tonight,' said a voice from the doorway, 'may I borrow it, Kitty? It's so beautifully made.' It was Shirley, one of the American girls.

The girls at the exclusive boarding school in the Vienna Woods were getting ready for their regular Friday night dance.

'All hand-stitched,' said Kitty, as she pulled first one dress and then another out of the wardrobe, held it up, and looked at it critically. 'Excellent Hungarian dressmaking.'

'So, will you let me wear it this week?' asked Shirley again.

Mama, Papa and Polly Kratky, owners of the boarding school in Purkersdorf, Vienna Woods.

'Yes, if you like. But what should I wear?'

'What about your grey frock with the beaded collar?' she suggested.

Lily had dropped out of the conversation, and was making her own preparations for the dance. Although Kitty had met Lily when visiting her grandmother in the village of Kosice prior to coming to the school, and although they shared a room, there was always some slight coolness between them. Later Kitty would discover why.

'The grey frock with the beaded collar?' repeated Kitty. 'Yes, that might be nice. I'll try it on, and you tell me how I look.'

The school itself was a large, old white house—vaguely resembling a small castle. It was owned by the Kratky family. Mama and Papa Kratky managed the school, and their daughter Polly taught the fifteen girls in residence a range of languages and social skills. The school was preparing the girls (mostly aged 18 or 19) for entry into the Consular Academy in Vienna—which would then open the way to employment in the diplomatic service.

Kitty and Lily shared a double room that looked out over a vista of pine trees. It was like a small hotel room with flowered wallpaper, plainly furnished with two single beds, two desks and a single wardrobe. The whole building was set up like a large guesthouse with rooms for the girls, a big family room in which lessons were given, a large kitchen in which the girls learned to cook, and a separate dining room. Around the building was a huge yard, and beyond the yard the dark pine trees of the forest began.

Throughout the school that Friday evening the girls giggled and whispered as they hunted through their wardrobes looking for the right dress for the social event of the week. They were thinking about the boys from the University of Technology, the tall, handsome engineering students they would dance with that night.

As Shirley turned to leave the room with Kitty's blue and silver dress over her arm she saw Merle, another of the American girls, standing in the doorway. In the corridor behind her were several others girls.

'Do you think Kurt will be there tonight?' Shirley asked Merle.

Merle blushed but didn't reply.

'Of course he'll be there,' said Kitty with a laugh, 'and he will want to dance with Merle all night.'

Merle's blush turned a deeper red.

'And Hans will be there,' said one of the girls from the corridor. 'Oh, I do hope that Hans will be there.'

'And Freidrich,' said another.

'And Fritz,' said a third, and then they all broke in a gale of girlish laughter.

'Do you think Polly has a boyfriend?' asked Shirley, as the laughter died down.

This was a mystery they had all puzzled over every Friday evening. When Polly, their teacher, shepherded them into the ballroom, she always disappeared, only to return as the dance was coming to a close. Where was she in the meantime?

'Of course, she has a boyfriend,' said Lily, and then added with a conspiratorial whisper. 'Perhaps he's a married boyfriend, and that's why they can only meet on Friday nights at the hotel.'

'Do you think they ...?' began Merle, and then blushed and didn't finish her question.

'Of course they do!' replied Lily with cynical superiority.

'But we've never seen her with anyone,' Kitty pointed out.

'Perhaps Lily's right,' said one of the girls in the corridor. 'Perhaps he's married and they can only meet in secret, and that's why we've never seen him.'

'One Friday,' said Kitty with a cheeky smile, 'someone should follow her when she leaves the ballroom and see where she goes.'

'I'm not leaving the dance,' Merle said.

'Not if Kurt's there, you mean,' added Shirley, and Merle blushed again.

If the girls had followed their teacher on a Friday night they would have discovered that she was attending secret meetings of the Austrian Nazi Party, held on the top floor of the hotel.

But they were not thinking about politics. Like so many teenagers before and since, they had no interest in politics at all.

The school was on the edge of the small village of

Purkersdorf, and at six thirty—at the same moment that Austrian President Miklas was on the phone to Adolf Hitler—the girls were boarding a train into the city of Vienna where each week they attended the dance at a small, exclusive hotel called *Hubner In Hitzing*.

The electric train clicked rhythmically over the rails. Their heads and their conversations were empty of politics and filled only with dresses and dances and boys. The rail journey would take, they knew, some one and a half hours. At eight o'clock they would arrive at the railway station at Hitzing, a suburb of Vienna. As they walked out of the pedestrian underpass from the railway station they would be able to see the elegant two story hotel that was their destination on the other side of the square. The boys from the University would already be there, waiting for them.

'Girls, stop fidgeting,' snapped Polly, as Kitty and her friends whispered and giggled. Polly was never particularly friendly with the girls. She was somewhat aloof and cool, with tendency to be secretive and quite abrupt in her dealings with her students. The girls thought of her as a very plain young woman with short brown hair—not at all pretty—and lucky to have a boyfriend (if, indeed, she did have one).

Kitty had checked her appearance half a dozen times in the mirror before they left the school, and she knew she looked pretty in her grey dress with the beaded collar. A number of times she glanced enviously at her roommate Lily—she was so petite and blonde and so very pretty. She patted a stray hair into place, and leaned over to whisper quietly to the other Jewish girl in the group, Eva Perl. Eva was something of a loner at the school, an awkward girl she spoke German with a heavy Polish accent.

Then Shirley was tapping Kitty on the elbow and leaning over to whisper, 'Did you know that Kurt and Fritz are cousins?'

'No, I didn't,' replied Kitty, 'they certainly don't look alike.'

And soon they were deep in conversation about the boys who would be at the dance.

As the train rattled on through the darkness, the fallen Austrian Chancellor, Kurt Von Schuschnigg, went on the radio ordering Austrian troops to offer no resistance if the Germans invaded. Later he was to say that he had issued that order only to avoid bloodshed. But when it was broadcast, it caused jubilation among Austrian Nazis, and fear in the hearts of those who knew what Nazi rule would mean.

The train from the Vienna Woods into the city was crowded, and the journey felt, to the impatient schoolgirls, as if it was going on forever. But at exactly eight o'clock the train pulled up at Hitzing railway station, and the girls enthusiastically piled out.

But when they trooped out of the station through the pedestrian underpass they stopped in shock and bewilderment. The sight that met their eyes was not what they had expected. Instead of the usual Friday night traffic, the square was packed, shoulder to shoulder, with a restless angry crowd of people, hundreds of people, many of them carrying flaming torches, and most of them chanting 'Heil Hitler! Heil Hitler!'

The fifteen schoolgirls huddled together, frightened by the tension, the angry voices, and the feeling that, at any moment, violence might break out.

The crowd surged around the square, defying anyone to try to stop them, or to call them unpatriotic. The angry demonstration had blocked the square to all vehicles. The noise, the crush of bodies, and the flickering torch light in the darkness gave the scene the feeling of a medieval witch burning crowd, baying for a victim.

'Heil Hitler! Heil Hitler!' they chanted.

Someone in that milling crowd recognised Polly Kratky and came hurrying across to the little group. 'Heil Hitler!' he said, making the Nazi salute.

To the girls' surprise and horror, their teacher smiled broadly, raised her right arm in the Nazi salute, and responded with her own enthusiastic 'Heil Hitler!' Soon Polly and the man were deep in conversation. As he turned back towards the milling throng, Polly told her girls, 'It's wonderful! Simply wonderful!'

The schoolgirls were puzzled as well as frightened. They had their best dresses on. Were the boys from the university waiting for them? Would the dance still be held? What was going on?

Eva Perl grabbed Kitty's arm. Kitty could feel her trembling.

'What on earth's going on?' whispered Eva.

'I don't know,' said Kitty. 'I don't know.'

The whole area was filled with flickering yellow light from the mass of flaming torches carried by the crowd.

'It's just a sea of flames,' Merle whispered in a horrified voice.

The chanting was relentless: 'Heil Hitler! Heil Hitler!' It was a cool night, and many in the crowd were wearing overcoats over their business suits or working clothes. Some coats flapped open, casting large, black shadows like bat wings. A few of them were wearing uniforms—the black shirts of the Nazi *Schutzstaffel*, or SS. The flaming torches crackled and leaped into the air.

Polly Kratky turned to the fifteen schoolgirls who were huddling together, and cried, 'Hitler is coming!' Her eyes were alight, and her face was jubilant. The girls felt confused. They didn't know what to do, and didn't really understand what was happening. They huddled close to each other for comfort in stunned silence, the strain showing on their young faces.

'Don't you understand?' Polly cried enthusiastically. 'Hitler is coming!'

Some of the girls realised then that their teacher expected them to be pleased, and so they tried to smile and pretend they were happy to hear the news, although why it was supposed to be so wonderful, or what it might mean for them, they still didn't understand.

'I'll come back in a minute, girls,' said Polly Kratky abruptly, and she hurried off to talk to someone in that swirling, aggressive crowd, returning a few minutes later.

'There'll be no dance tonight,' said Polly, rejoining the girls. 'We will stay here for a little while, and then we'll return to the school.'

For half an hour they stood on the edge of that surging crowd, while Polly dashed off to speak to this one and that one, and to join in the chanting of 'Heil Hitler! Heil Hitler!'

Around the square Kitty Kalafoni could see red and black Nazi swastika flags that were now flying from buildings and flagpoles—flags she had never seen in that square before.

The Nazi Party—or National Socialist German Workers Party, to give its full name—had been formed by Adolf Hitler in 1919. It was a highly disciplined, militant party passionately committed to pan-German nationalism. What Kitty saw in the square that night was the power of the aggressive, well-organized Nazi Party machine to mobilise its members, and intimidate its enemies.

At half past eight, Polly Kratky, concerned that there might be violent resistance to the Nazi take-over, led her party of schoolgirls back onto the railway platform, where they caught the first train that would return them to Purkersdorf, and the boarding school.

As the train carried them back through the darkness, the girls were filled with a jumble of conflicting emotions. Their only thought was: 'What else would the night bring? What surprises might it still hold?'

As the train rattled through the darkness, at exactly 8:45 that night, Hitler issued the invasion order. Soon German troops were pouring over the border. Hitler's stormtroopers swept rapidly through Austria, finding no resistance—the local Nazi party had done its job, and power was theirs for the taking.

Fifteen teenage schoolgirls sat in their seats in that rocking, swaying train, too stunned by the night's events to say anything. The train was packed tightly with passengers, all of them talking about what was happening, and what was about to happen. Kitty sat between her American friends and they clutched each other's arms during that hour and a half long return journey. Eva Perl sat by herself in a corner of the crowded railway carriage, a plain, lumpish girl trembling with nervous agitation. Only Lily, Kitty noticed, seemed to be accepting the events of the night calmly and quietly. She sat upright in her seat, her face composed, staring at the reflections of the passengers in the windows of the carriage as the train roared through the night.

It was after ten o'clock when the weary girls—exhausted by the emotional turmoil as much as anything else—tumbled out of the train. To their amazement they found the scene in Vienna was repeated, on a smaller scale, in the little village of Purkersdorf. The streets were filled with people, many of them giving the Nazi salute, and many others shouting 'Heil Hitler! Heil Hitler!' The railway station itself was flying a swastika from its flagpole.

Polly didn't let them linger in the village, or on the main road, the Linzerstrasse, where the biggest crowds were, but walked them up the hill from the station to their school.

But that night still held one further, unpleasant, shock for them. Ten minutes after leaving the village railway station, as the school came in sight, they saw that a red and black Nazi swastika flag was hanging from every window of the building in which they lived.

'They can't have found so many flags in just a few hours,'

Kitty whispered to Shirley. 'They must have been planning for this for ages.'

'They must have hung out the flags when they heard the news on the radio,' responded the American, in a hushed and horrified tone. 'Mama and Papa Kratky must have done this. They're so nice—why would they do this?

'Hurry up you two,' snapped Polly sharply. 'Get to your rooms and get to bed.'

3

KITTY FOUND IT HARD to sleep that night. Long after the Slovakian girl in the other bed had fallen asleep and was snoring quietly, Kitty lay awake staring at the ceiling, feeling the fear growing within, feeling confused, frightened and uncomprehending of all that had happened.

She remembered the previous January when Polly had taken the girls skiing at Schneeberg in the Austrian Alps. On that occasion people had greeted each other with the words, 'Heil Hitler!'

When Kitty had asked Polly, 'What's going on?', Polly had replied, 'Oh, well, we're over a thousand metres above sea level here, and above a thousand metres you can say whatever you like.'

Kitty had thought it a strange reply at the time, and, thinking back, she realised that Polly was just making an excuse to cover the fact that other members of the Austrian Nazi Party had recognised her as a party member, and organizer, and were greeting her with the party salute.

As the events of the previous January came back to her, Kitty made herself think about the beautiful snow, and the skiing, and the ski hut the girls had stayed in—anything to get the disturbing scenes of the last few hours out of her mind. But that night the first seeds of bitterness and anger were planted in Kitty's heart—seeds that were to grow over the turbulent years ahead.

Eventually sleep found her, but she slept restlessly and was troubled by nightmares.

The next morning Kitty gathered with the other girls for breakfast in the dining room. All the talk was about the strange events of the night before. The radio was turned up loudly, and all the girls listened to the news, trying to take in the significance of the events they were caught up in. And then every voice in the room fell silent as Polly Kratky entered.

In amazement the girls stared at their teacher—now wearing the brown uniform of the Nazi SA—the *Sturmabteilung* or "brownshirts".

'What are you gaping at girls,' snapped Polly. 'Get on with your breakfast.'

Slowly the teenagers turned back to the table, too surprised, too stunned, to say anything.

She actually looked rather impressive in the uniform, but also rather masculine, the girls thought, and Polly was clearly filled with pride—in fact, more than pride, arrogance.

'Oh, and one other thing,' Polly continued. 'Kitty Kalafoni and Eva Perl—you two Jews can bunk in together. Kalafoni you are to move out of your room immediately after breakfast, and move in with Perl. And it would be best for the rest of you girls to have as little to do with the Jews as possible.' Kitty could hear a change in Polly's voice—there was a new, more severe coldness, a brusqueness, she had not heard before.

After breakfast, Kitty felt emotionally numb as she silently packed up her clothes and belongings and moved into Eva Perl's room. The girl who had been sharing with Eva swapped over, and moved into the room Kitty had shared with the Slovakian girl. After all the clothes had been moved over, Kitty sat on the end of her bed. Eva sat down beside her and held her hands. The two girls were terrified.

Later that day Hitler announced the *Anschluss*, or union, of Germany and Austria.

The following day, Sunday March 13, 1938 Kitty and Eva Perl found that they were expected to eat their breakfast separately from the others, in a corner of the small dining room. Polly Kratky made it clear the other girls shouldn't mix with them.

The two Jewish girls were still shaken and terrified, but for the others, including the Americans, the initial shock had worn off, and they were happy and bubbling again. When Polly entered in her striking uniform they gathered around her and listened intently as she talked excitedly to them. Kitty and Eva looked at each other—whatever was going on was clearly for non-Jews only.

'But...we're all friends...' murmured Eva glumly.

Kitty said nothing, but she pondered the fun they had all had together, how they had been like sisters to each other, and how overnight the world seemed to have changed.

After breakfast the phone rang. Herr Kratky called out, 'Kitty—a phone call for you. It's your father, from Budapest.'

'Papa, you'll never guess what's happened...' gushed Kitty as she picked up the phone.

'We've heard,' interrupted her father. 'It's all over the news. Are you all right? What's happening to you?'

'Yes...yes, I'm fine. Our teacher here, Miss Polly, she's wearing a uniform now. Papa, she's a Nazi!'

Kitty heard her father turn away from the telephone and say

something to her mother, then he asked, 'Are they still feeding you, and looking after you?'

'Oh, yes. I'm now sharing a room with another Jewish girl—and the other girls have been told not to talk to us. But...well, that's all.'

'We need to get you home, Kitty,' said her father sternly. 'The border between Austria and Hungary has been closed, but just as soon as it's open again, we'll get you home.'

'Yes please,' whispered Kitty urgently. 'I want to come home.'

'If they let you go into Vienna again,' her father continued, speaking quickly, knowing the phone line might not stay open for long, 'there is a family you should visit. Their name is Farago. Your uncle's family on your mother's side—I suppose they're cousins actually. Just in case things get worse and there's trouble, they would help you. There are three of them, a baby, or a little boy he would be by now, a boy named John, as well as Mr and Mrs Farago. You go and see them. If I have difficulty getting you out, they might be able to help. Get a piece of paper to write on and I will tell you the address.'

'Yes, Papa.'

'And I'll telephone every day or two to see how you're getting on.'

'Yes, Papa.'

'And I'll get you home with us just as soon as I can.'

'Oh, yes please, Papa.'

As Kitty walked back to her room clutching the address her father had given her tightly in her fist, she felt shaken by the fear she could hear in her father's voice.

About the middle of the morning Polly began rushing around gathering up the girls.

'We're going to see Hitler!' she shouted. 'He's coming. His car will pass by very shortly. Come on, come on—I want you all out on the road to see him. And I'll find you flags that you can wave.'

The Jewish girls Kitty and Eva hung back, uncertain as to what they should do.

'You two Jews,' said Polly sharply, 'you come too. It will do you good to see Hitler. We need the biggest crowd possible on the side of the road. Anyway,' she added over her shoulder, 'I can't leave you alone in the house, so come on. Quickly now.'

Kitty and Eva followed her.

A straggling line of schoolgirls followed their young teacher to the side of the Linzerstrasse—the main road that ran past the front of the house. Flags were handed out, and they were told to line up and wait. Everyone from the village was there—even the old people and the babies. Purkersdorf was only a small town, but the entire population had gathered along both sides of the road. People were milling around and gathering in groups, lining up at the edge of the highway with their neighbours and friends, chatting excitedly, waiting for the passing cavalcade—waiting to see the face of the man who had tied the fate of Austria to that of Germany.

The sense of anticipation was electric. Kitty could feel the excitement around about her, although she felt strangely detached from it. This, she knew, was not for her. It was not for Jews. But she too wanted to see the man who was coming, the man who could capture Austria without firing a shot, the man whose very presence meant that Jews had to be segregated away from non-Jews. What was he really like, Kitty wondered?

As the hour crept towards noon the sound of motor cycles could be heard in the distance. A few minutes later the escort of motor cycles, tanks and cars swept around the bend in the road, followed by a cavalcade of half a dozen cars. And there—in the midst of that fleet of large, black cars—was the open limousine carrying the *Führer*.

As they approached the village the cavalcade slowed down, and Hitler stood up in the back of the limousine. He raised his right arm in the Nazi salute—responding to the wild shouts, cheers and salutes from the crowd along the roadside.

Adolf Hitler had been born in 1889 in the Austria to which he was now returning as triumphant conqueror. Twenty years before his army swept across the German-Austrian border he had been an art student in Vienna, beginning to form his ideas about "racial purity" based on his steadily growing hatred for Jews, Slavs and other "non-Germans". In the bitter, defeated Germany of the years after the First World War, Hitler had formed his Nazi Party and begun his march to power. He whipped huge crowds to a frenzy with his powerful, violent speeches—and ordered his brown-shirted, swastika-wearing followers to attack his political enemies. Since becoming dictator of Germany in 1933 he had turned that country into a powerful war machine. In 1936 he had broken the Treaty of Versailles by sending his troops to occupy the Rhineland. And now he was becoming impatient to see his Third Reich begin the conquest of Europe.

Kitty stood there glumly, frozen to the spot. In her hand was the flag Polly had given her to wave. She forgot to wave it—all she could do was to stare at the man in the uniform, standing in the back of the gleaming, black limousine.

He was less than six feet away from her. She remembered for the rest of her life the face she saw that day. He was wearing a military uniform with a peaked cap. Escaping from underneath the cap was a shock of unruly black hair. On the upper lip was the famous black, bristling moustache. As for the face itself, it was pale, so pale as to be startlingly white. And it had the soft, puffy appearance of a face that was used to self-indulgence.

None of the girls at the school discussed their reaction to Adolf Hitler—at least not with Kitty, not then, and not later.

They appeared to be stunned into silence. If they had any negative thoughts they would never have dared to utter them for fear of reaching Polly's ears.

Once the cavalcade had disappeared into the distance, they were marched back to the school. Kitty wondered as they went through the gates how she, a stunned, uncomprehending 18-year-old Jewish girl, had come to be living in a school run by Nazis.

4

AFTER SHE HAD finished primary school, Kitty's parents had sent her to a private Jewish high school. She graduated after four years there. From this there were three educational possibilities: the lyceum, from which it was not possible go to university; the gymnasium, which provided matriculation and entry to university; and the commercial academy, which provided entry into commerce and the arts. Kitty and her parents decided on the commercial academy. Her ambition was to work as a secretary in the diplomatic corps. The best preparation for this was a college in Vienna called the Consular Academy, which taught languages and provided training for diplomatic service. Graduation from the Viennese Consular Academy meant automatic employment in an embassy or consulate.

In September of 1937, at the start of the European school year, Kitty's mother went to Vienna and arranged for Kitty to attend the boarding school at Purkersdorf to prepare for entry into the Consular Academy. She chose the school because the building and the setting were so utterly delightful. Unknown to her, the school she found was the only boarding school in Vienna run by closet Nazis.

Later Kitty realised that the parents of her American friends were Nazi sympathisers who had sent their daughters to Purkersdorf knowing full well who was in charge of the school and where their true loyalties lay. This did nothing to weaken Kitty's affection for Shirley, Merle and the others—it was the parents, Kitty decided, and not the girls themselves, who were enthusiasts for Hitler's regime. The only exception to this among the girls appeared to be Lily, who grew to have a personal commitment to the Nazi ideology, and seemed to take real pleasure in the Nazi take-over. But although the American girls did not personally believe in the anti-Jewish philosophy of the Nazis, they were intimidated by Polly, in her SA uniform, and kept their distance from Kitty and Eva.

Kitty had enjoyed her time in the beautiful old building outside the city, in the Vienna Woods. It was such a small and intimate boarding school with never more than 15 to 20 girls at any one time, from many parts of Europe as well as the United States. All of the girls were foreigners: there was not one Austrian student. At this international school the instruction was in German—but Kitty had grown up bi-lingual, speaking both German and the Hungarian language, Magyar. Most of the instruction consisted of learning languages (Italian, French and German) but in many ways it focused more on developing the social skills and graces needed in the diplomatic service— which is why the girls attended the opera and the ballet, and went to balls and dances.

In the middle of the week following the *Anschluss* Polly once again took the schoolgirls into the city of Vienna where Hitler was scheduled to make another public appearance, and, once again, she insisted that the Jewish girls come with them. Kitty thought this might be an opportunity for her to visit the Farago family, as her father had suggested.

'Miss?' she asked Polly.

'Yes,' replied the teacher, who no longer addressed the Jewish girls by name.

'Why are we going into the city?'

'Hitler is to make an appearance in the city square. You will get to see Hitler again. Satisfied?'

'Afterwards Miss, may I go and visit my relatives?'

'I didn't know you had any relatives in Vienna.'

'My father suggested I should visit them as soon as possible. May I?'

'I suppose so. It might be a useful activity. It might stop you looking miserable all the time.'

This time they caught the electric train to a station in the heart of the city. From there Miss Kratky led the way to Karlsplatz, a large, central square already packed with people. As they pushed their way into the crowd Kitty's attention was caught by hand-painted cardboard signs that had appeared in the windows of shops and cafes: "Dogs and Jews not allowed," the signs read. Kitty was shocked. Her sense of the danger all around her became sharper.

Eva grabbed Kitty's hand and pointed at one of the signs.

'I know,' said Kitty, 'they're all over the place.'

'But how can they?' mumbled Eva. 'How can they say that? How can they?'

Kitty did not reply. Both girls knew that some of the signs were just there to please their new Nazi masters—but others were there because it allowed the shopkeepers to say what they had been wanting to say for a long time.

The crowds in the plaza were all gazing towards a first floor hotel balcony that was draped with red and black swastika flags.

The plaza was packed and more people kept arriving all the time. Kitty found herself squeezed in tightly by the restless, excited crowd. There were several thousand people in the plaza that afternoon.

Eventually Hitler appeared on the balcony of the Hotel Bristol, and the crowd went wild. For minutes on end they cheered, saluted, and cried out, 'Heil Hitler! Heil Hitler!' The German dictator acknowledged their salutes with his own, and for some minutes he stood on the flag-draped balcony smiling and saluting. Finally, after what seemed to Kitty to be an eternity of being surrounded by ear-splitting cheering and chanting, Hitler went back inside.

'I'm disappointed,' said Polly, as the crowd began to break up. 'I'd so hoped he would give a speech. I've never heard him speak, except on radio.'

As the crowd rapidly began to thin out, Polly announced, 'Kalafoni, you may go and visit your relatives now. You other girls, come with me.'

Leaving the others behind, Kitty caught a tram to the Mariahilfe Strasse where her relatives, the Faragos, lived. When she reached their street she walked down the pavement, checking the building numbers, and glancing from time to time at the scrap of paper in her hand. When she found the building she wanted, and the apartment number she was looking for, she knocked nervously at the apartment door.

'Yes?' said the man who opened the door just a crack.

'I'm Kitty Kalafoni,' she said, 'Papa told me to...'

The man opened the door wider, stepped out, and looked nervously up and down the hallway.

'Yes, yes,' he said hurriedly, as he grabbed Kitty's arm and pulled her inside, 'you'd better come in quickly. You might be attacked on the street if people see that you're coming to visit us. All our neighbours know we are Jews.'

Introductions were soon made. What struck Kitty was how nervous they looked—the young couple and the small boy in the cot. They were shaking with fear.

'I don't understand how you can dare to walk the streets,' said the young mother, as she checked the infant in his cot.

'Just the thought of a Jewish girl walking the streets on her own,' said her husband, 'is terrifying—simply terrifying. We never leave the apartment these days—we just don't go out. It's not safe. Have you seen the signs in the shop windows: "Dogs and Jews not allowed"?'

Kitty said she had, and then asked them for news she could take back to her family in Budapest.

'Tell them we're getting out—just as soon as we can.'

As the young woman went into the kitchen to make Kitty a cup of hot chocolate, her husband leaned forward and said earnestly, 'You shouldn't have come here. It's not safe. Don't come back—please don't come back.'

'Is it so very dangerous, then?'

'Yes! Yes!'

'And you are going to leave?'

'Of course. As soon as possible. We're making arrangements to send John to either Denmark or Holland, and we will follow him as soon as we can get travel papers.'

'What will happen to me?' she asked.

'You have your Hungarian passport, so you're all right. Nothing can happen to you.'

When it was time to leave, the Faragos hugged Kitty and wept and told her to take great care of herself.

Kitty left their house that afternoon more shaken than ever, and more anxious than ever to get out of the dangers of Austria and back to the safety and security of her home in Budapest.

All attempts at lessons at the boarding school came to a halt. Polly was missing from the house most days, rushing in and out of Vienna on Nazi business. As a long-standing member of the Nazi party she had come into her own, now that the party had assumed power.

The girls at the school had time on their hands. They sat around sewing or reading, so Frau Kratky said, 'All right, come into the kitchen and I will teach you girls to cook.' And for many days after that fifteen girls crowded into the large, old Austrian kitchen to have cooking lessons from Mama Kratky. She was a small, plump jovial Austrian woman, and Kitty would often look at her cheerful face during a cooking lesson and wonder how this woman could accept the Nazi philosophy and drape her home in Nazi flags. Papa Kratky was just as much a puzzle. He was a placid, comfortable man who was putting on weight because he was too fond of sweet Viennese pastries. Why would such a man want to cheer the arrival of Adolf Hitler, Kitty wondered?

Kitty's father took to ringing her every second day. Each call was only a few minutes long, but that was enough to reassure him that his daughter was still alive, still surviving. And it was long enough to alarm Kitty each time they spoke, alarm her at the nervousness and anxiety she could hear in his voice. They spoke in Hungarian, which gave them some privacy, although Kitty noticed that the Kratky family scowled at her angrily whenever they couldn't understand what she was saying.

In April, almost a month after the *Anschluss*, the Austrian-Hungarian border was re-opened. Immediately Kitty's father began arranging for her return to Budapest. The Kratkys seemed pleased to know that she would be going.

Kitty returned to her room to find her Jewish room mate, Eva Perl, packing a suitcase.

'My bus ticket has arrived,' she explained, without turning around. 'It was in this morning's post from my father. I'm to catch a bus for Poland this afternoon.'

'It's very sudden.'

'I think the post was held up at the border. I should have got the letter two days ago.'

Then she turned towards Kitty and said, 'I'll miss you.'

Kitty hugged her and said, 'And I'll miss you, too.'

'You be careful. Look after yourself, and get out of here as quickly as you can.'

Kitty promised that she would be very careful not to say or do the wrong thing, until she was also able to get away.

As Eva fastened the catches on her suitcase she said, 'Will we ever see each other again?'

'Of course we will! Some day. When all this is over. Hitler will have to stop soon. Other countries won't let him get away with too much.'

'Hush! You mustn't say such things...not out loud. Imagine what Polly would say if she heard you!'

Kitty had the room to herself that night, and two days later her father rang again.

'Please, miss,' said Kitty when she got off the phone, 'Papa has made arrangements for me to go home.'

'Just go,' replied Polly, 'we just want you out of here. So, just go.'

The following day Polly escorted Kitty into Vienna on a train, and left her at the bus terminal in Karlsplatz, where a month earlier they had seen Hitler saluting the crowd from a hotel balcony. Polly Kratky's last words to Kitty were, 'Tell your father he still has to pay for the full term despite your early withdrawal from the school.' With that she turned and was gone.

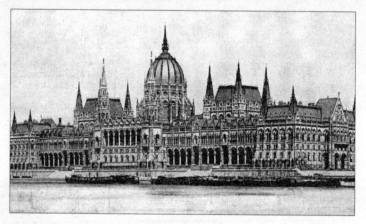

Budapest.

5

WHILE KITTY WAS waiting for the bus to Budapest, surrounded by a restless crowd of people, all, it seemed, keen to get out of Austria, she was approached by a man.

'Excuse me, miss?' he said.

She looked up to see a stranger, a young man of about 25 years of age. He was speaking to her in Hungarian.

'I noticed that you only have one bag.'

Kitty looked down at the solitary suitcase at her feet, and nodded.

'I wonder,' continued the young man, 'if you'd mind taking an extra case on the bus for me. You see, I have too much luggage, but you're well under the luggage limit, and they'll let you take an extra case.' The expression on his face was almost pleading with her.

Kitty felt uncomfortable. It was hard to say no to such a personable young man who was pleading with her, but she was nervous, and the last thing she wanted to do was carry someone else's luggage across the border. What if the border guards searched the luggage, what would they find inside this case she was being asked to take? Valuables of some sort? Contraband? Jewellery? Mink?

As Kitty hesitated the young man spoke again. 'You're such an innocent looking girl,' he said, 'I'm sure they'd never search your luggage.'

That made her even more nervous.

Eventually she stammered, 'No...no, I can't. I'm sorry...I just can't. I'm a young girl on my own. What if they stop me, what if they search my luggage? No...please don't ask me again, I just can't help you.'

When the time came to board the bus Kitty found that it was packed, mainly with foreign Jews who had been working or holidaying in Austria at the time of the *Anschluss*. After lengthy delays the bus rumbled away with its heavy load, towards the Austrian-Hungarian border.

At the border the vehicle was stopped and the passengers all made to get off the bus. Their passports and other papers were examined by German soldiers, who also searched the bus and opened all the luggage. In the turmoil Kitty never saw what happened to the young man with the contraband suitcase.

Kitty arrived back in Budapest in early April, 1938. She was met at the bus terminal in the city centre by her father, Aladar Kalafoni, and taken straight back to the family apartment at 9 Academia Street, Lipotváros, in the old Inner City.

Later, when she was safely home Kitty told her father the story of the young man at the bus depot, and he said, 'Good girl. I'm glad you didn't take it. You did the right thing in refusing. Well done.'

Kitty's mother, Adele (known as Ada), hugged her and wept and said how worried they had both been about her. Ada was not normally particularly affectionate or expressive, but Kitty was an only child, and her mother's concern for her was, on this occasion, genuine and heartfelt.

Kitty was happy to be home again.

Close by their apartment block were the House of Parliament and the Hungarian Academy of Sciences. From their balcony Kitty could look across the Danube to the historic buildings that covered the steep hills on the western side of the river. As April warmed into June a golden summer began—the last peaceful summer that Europe was to see for six long, dark years. Kitty spent that summer seeing her friends, simply glad to be home again.

CHAPTER 5

Budapest was the capital and largest city in Hungary, lying on both banks of the Danube in the north of the country. In 1873, the three adjoining cities of Buda, Pest and Obuda, united with Margaret Island to form Budapest. On the western bank of the Danube stood what used to be the city of Buda with its historic buildings, beautiful old houses and steep wooded hills. The Royal Palace, which included the remains of an ancient fort, stood on the top of Castle Hill in the centre of Buda. It was in Buda that Kitty had been born in 1920. But now she and her family lived on the eastern side of the river, as did most of the population, in what had once been Pest. Containing the House of Parliament, the commercial centre and the old Inner City, called Lipotváros, Pest stood on a series of plateaus. Eight bridges across the Danube linked the two parts of the city.

In the weeks that followed, life returned to normal for the Kalafoni family. Father went to work each day in his well-paid job as a chartered accountant, and the parties and social life of Budapest continued as busily as ever.

Aladar and Ada Kalafoni were Jews, but not particularly religious Jews. They attended synagogue only once a year, and were quite relaxed about Jewish dietary laws. They had married young, and continued to behave like a young couple for most of their married life. They were great party-goers, and their lives revolved around entertainment and the pursuit of leisure and pleasure.

But, somehow, life was now not entirely normal. The swastika cast its large, dark shadow over Hungary. Constantly, in the back of everyone's mind, was the knowledge that Nazi troops were at the Austrian-Hungarian border—about an hour's drive from Budapest.

Every night Kitty and her parents gathered around the radio

to hear the latest news of Hitler's activities, and his increasingly bombastic threats. From Germany came the repeated lies that there had been no 'invasion' of Austria—German troops had been dispatched only in answer to 'urgent' appeals from the newly formed Austrian government (formed late on that Friday night, after the dismissal of Kurt von Schuschnigg as Chancellor of Austria). By the time of Kitty's return the news had already leaked out that mass arrests were going on throughout Austria. Within a month there were 79,000 political prisoners in Vienna alone—arrested on the grounds that they were regarded as 'unreliables' by their new German masters.

On April 10, 1938 Austrians voted in a plebiscite on their *Anschluss* ('union') with Germany. A whirlwind campaign by Hitler, and a flood of Nazi propaganda, led up to this vote. The thrust of their campaign was an attempt to re-write history by claiming the *Anschluss* had been made necessary by the incompetence and dishonesty of the democratically elected government of Austria that they had overthrown. Those opposing the *Anschluss* were denied the right to campaign. The combination of Hitler's emotional speeches and the flood of Nazi propaganda (together with the suppression of all opposition) won the day, and the plebiscite was carried by a large *Ja* ('Yes') vote.

Many Catholics in this overwhelmingly Catholic country were undoubtedly swayed by a widely publicized statement of Cardinal Innitzer welcoming Nazism to Austria and urging a *Ja* vote. A few months later, on October 8, the cardinal's palace, opposite St Stephen's Cathedral in Vienna, was trashed by Nazi thugs. Too late, the Cardinal had discovered what Nazism really was, and had spoken out in a sermon against Nazi persecution of his church.

6

THE PERSECUTION OF Austrian Jews began. Hundreds of Jews, men and women, were picked up off the streets and compelled to work cleaning public latrines, and the toilets at the SS barracks. While they worked, on their hands and knees, jeering soldiers stood around and crowds gathered to taunt them. Tens of thousands of Jews were jailed, and their possessions seized. According to American journalist William Shirer, perhaps half of Vienna's 180,000 Jews managed, by the time the Second World War started, to purchase their freedom to emigrate by handing over what they owned to the Nazis.

It was no longer possible to make contact with the Farago family by telephone, and Kitty and her parents simply had to hope they had been among those to make it out of Austria alive.

So it was that Austria, as Austria, ceased to exist (at least for the time being) and it became a province of Greater Germany—Hitler's glorious Third Reich. Without firing a shot and without interference from Britain, France, or Russia, whose military forces could have overwhelmed him, Hitler had added seven million people to the Reich and gained a strategic position of immense value to his future plans.

The Nazi occupation of Austria meant that Czechoslovakia was surrounded by German troops on three sides. Hitler's second in command, Hermann Goering, kept issuing statements insisting that Czechoslovakia had nothing to fear from Germany, that the entry of the Reich's troops into Austria was 'nothing more than a family affair' and that Hitler wanted to improve relations with Prague.

Constant reassurances that Czechoslovakia had nothing to

fear from Germany made the Czechoslovaks very nervous. All of Kitty's father's family were still living in Slovakia at the time.

Kitty's father would express his concerns by muttering, after each radio news bulletin, 'If Czechoslovakia falls, can Hungary be far behind?'

When Aladar Kalafoni and his friends sat around in the apartment, drinking coffee and wine late at night, their conversation often came back to the fact that Hitler had seized Austria while Britain, France, Russia and the League of Nations had done nothing to stop him. Newspaper articles were read and re-read looking for any sign that the powerful nations of Europe might offer some resistance to Hitler's relentless aggression. Speaking in the House of Commons, British Prime Minister Neville Chamberlain had rejected the suggestion that Britain should give a guarantee to come to the aid of Czechoslovakia in case she were attacked. Then he went further, and also rejected the proposal that Britain might support France if the French were called upon to fulfil their obligations under the Franco-Czech mutual defence agreement.

As the storm clouds gathered Aladar Kalafoni decided the only way to protect his family would be for them all to 'convert' to Roman Catholicism. He went to see a local priest who agreed that in return for a generous 'donation' he would take the three of them through catechism classes and baptize them as adult converts—as Catholics. Each week the three of them would go to their religious instruction classes. Years later Kitty could remember nothing of what she learned in those classes. After several months they were privately baptized by the priest, and then handed their precious pieces of paper—certificates declaring them to be Roman Catholics.

In the end those certificates proved to be worthless. The Nazis, it later proved, were not interested in certificates. To them, Jews were Jews—and belonged in extermination camps.

As the shadow of the swastika grew longer and darker there were urgent letters, followed by telegrams, from Aladar Kalafoni's cousin who was living in New York. He had gone to America after the First World War, done well in business and become wealthy. He wanted cousin Aladar to join him in America with his family. As a chartered accountant, he assured Aladar, he would quickly find work, and a generous salary, in the New World.

The family discussed the possibility of emigrating to America over their evening meal.

After all the pros and cons had been weighed up Kitty's father shrugged his shoulders and said, 'How can I? I can't speak English. And what about grandmother? She would never cope in New York. What could we do with her?' At that time Kitty's maternal grandmother, Gizella Schossberger, lived with them in their Budapest apartment.

A long silence followed, then he shrugged his shoulders again and said, 'We will survive—somehow.' The next day he wrote a letter to his cousins in New York passing on this decision. 'We are optimists,' he wrote, 'we will survive.'

When their reply finally arrived it was brief: 'Optimists don't survive,' they wrote, 'only pessimists survive.'

And so Kitty and her family stayed in Hungary, with a growing unease that the Nazi jackboot was getting closer and closer.

The nightly radio news broadcasts were becoming steadily more ominous. Hitler exploited the existence of a German minority in Czechoslovakia to generate an artificial crisis that might justify his invasion of the country. While Hitler pressed his allies—the Sudeten Germans within Czechoslovakia—to make more and more extravagant demands, he laid his secret plans: to destroy the Czechoslovak state and absorb its territories and inhabitants into the Third Reich. Encouraged by the German warlord, for that was what Hitler had now become, the Sudeten Germans demanded complete self-rule.

Hitler threatened war with Czechoslovakia if the demand was not met.

Desperate to avoid armed conflict, British Prime Minister Neville Chamberlain met with the German dictator at his Berchtesgaden retreat on September 15, 1938. Hitler demanded that the ethnic Germans living in Czechoslovakia 'return' to the Reich. Chamberlain flew back to England convinced he had Hitler's promise to seek a peaceful solution to the situation. The German dictator now began looking for allies to help him carve Czechoslovakia into pieces. He looked first to Hungary. On September 20 Hitler met Hungarian Prime Minister Imredy and Foreign Minister de Kanya to urge them to demand the return to Hungary of that part of the Czech territory in which Hungary had an historic interest. Hungarians were another minority ethnic group within Czechoslovakia, and Hitler wanted to use them to create a diversion while he planned to absorb the whole country into his growing empire.

All of this was followed with dread by the Kalafonis and countless other families in Hungary. They could see Hitler's rapacious appetite for conquest, and that their country was becoming allied with the Nazi leader.

Neville Chamberlain again met with Adolf Hitler on September 22 and 23 at Godesberg. The British Prime Minister presented the dictator with an Anglo-French peace plan that caved in to all his demands. But this was not what Hitler really wanted—his secret aim was still to destroy Czechoslovakia by military action. So Hitler increased his demands—he now insisted on immediate surrender of the disputed territory. Chamberlain, together with other national leaders, met Hitler a third time—in Munich on September 29 and 30. At this meeting the leaders of Britain and France agreed to Hitler's demand and signed the Munich Agreement, a pact that forced Czechoslovakia to give the

Sudetenland to Germany. Later that year, Hungary and Poland claimed other parts of Czechoslovakia. Chamberlain flew back to London waving a piece of paper—the Munich Agreement—which, he claimed, guaranteed 'peace in our time'.

Families in Budapest following these events on the radio and in their newspapers felt betrayed by Britain and France, and more insecure than ever in the face of Hitler's aggression. For Hungarian Jews there was also the unpalatable fact that their own government had taken the side of the Nazi dictator. This cast a further shadow over the future of Jews living in Hungary.

Among western leaders Winston Churchill alone seemed to understand the significance of the Munich Agreement. Speaking in the House of Commons, on October 5, 1938, he said: 'We are in the middle of a disaster of the first magnitude...All the countries of the Danube valley, will be drawn into the vast system of Nazi politics...And do not suppose this is the end. It is only the beginning...'

On the night of November 10, 1938 Germany saw the worst persecution so far against the Jews since the Nazis had come to power. This was *Crystalnacht*—the "Night of Broken Glass", a night of horror throughout Germany. Synagogues, Jewish homes and shops went up in flames, and Jewish men, women and children who tried to escape burning to death were shot as they fled. In that one night 815 shops were destroyed, 171 houses set on fire, 119 synagogues attacked (76 of them completely destroyed) and 20,000 Jews arrested.

As the news of this atrocity crackled over the small radio in the Kalafoni apartment, Kitty's father listened grimly. When the news broadcast came to an end he reached over and turned off the set, saying, 'Germany today—Hungary tomorrow.'

In March 1939 Germany seized the rest of Czechoslovakia. Slovakia became a separate republic under German control.

Hitler made Bohemia and Moravia a German protectorate. Having achieved his Czechoslovakian goal, Hitler now turned his eyes towards Poland, and began to plan the invasion that would begin the Second World War.

To anyone who saw where the German Army was now poised in Slovakia, Hitler's ambitions were obvious. And this time Britain and France were prepared to draw the line. Having failed Czechoslovakia they made it clear they would not fail Poland.

Speaking in the House of Commons on March 31, 1939, sixteen days after Hitler's army had marched into Prague, British Prime Minister Neville Chamberlain said that if Poland faced a military threat then the British government 'would feel bound to give the Polish Government all the support in their power.' He added that the French government had adopted the same view. Hitler had been warned. But he was not a man to be stopped by a warning.

As the month of August, 1939 began, Kitty father's announced that he intended to spend their savings on a special holiday in Italy. 'The Dolomites and Venice,' he said, 'we'll have a wonderful time. And it will take our minds off our troubles, and off the shadow hanging over our dear country. We might as well spend our money because we don't know what's going to happen.'

7

THAT AUTUMN THE weather was mild, and the holiday, in the glorious Italian alps, and then among the canals and splendid architecture of Venice, was to provide the family with their last time of real peace and happiness together.

Kitty's father Aladar had been born in Hungary. He was a country boy, who came to the city, met Kitty's mother, fell in love, and got married. He was descended from a long line of Sephardic Jews who had fled to Hungary from pogroms (persecutions) in Spain. Aladar's grandfather was an artist and engraver who designed the emblem of Aladar's hometown of Kassa, later renamed Kosice.

Kitty's mother, Ada, came from the well-to-do middle class Schossberger family in Budapest. They were married very young —just twenty and twenty-one at the time of their wedding. Kitty was a "honeymoon baby", born in the first year of the marriage. There were no other children, and Kitty grew up an only child.

On the one occasion each year when Ada and Aladar attended the synagogue, they made sure Kitty was well dressed. She wore new shoes and clothes that had been bought especially for the occasion. Her mother sat in the women's gallery while father sat downstairs with the men. While Kitty's parents didn't observe the Sabbath, or the dietary laws, her grandmother (her father's mother) did observe the kosher laws—very strictly.

Drama entered Kitty's life at the very beginning. Ada decided that she wasn't ready to have a baby so early in the marriage, and so she arranged for an abortion—at a time when this was still illegal in Hungary. Everything was organized and set up for the abortion in their apartment, which in those days was on the Buda side of the Danube. The abortionist, the woman who was to perform the procedure, was on her way from the other side of the city, from the Pest side of the river. However, she couldn't get across any of the bridges because of the Romanian troops who occupied much of Budapest at the time. This was in 1919, at the very beginning of the pregnancy. And so the abortion never happened.

Kitty's mother took little interest in her new baby, and Kitty was raised mainly by her grandmothers, and by the succession of maids her parents employed. All middle-class families in Europe at that time had a maid. There was also a nanny who cared for Kitty as a baby and toddler. But as Kitty grew, the nanny left, and her place was taken by the maids (and by the grandmothers). As she grew into a pretty little toddler Kitty became her father's spoiled favourite, and a close bond developed between them—closer than any bond Kitty ever developed with her mother.

Among Kitty's earliest memories (when they still lived on the Buda side of the city) are of having a peasant maid named Rosa caring for her. This maid was a special favourite of Kitty's, and was inclined to spoil the pretty little girl. Then Rosa got married, and young Kitty felt bereft, because her beloved Rosa had gone away.

As a child Kitty spent her summer holidays with Grandma Juliana Kalafoni in Czechoslovakia—holidays that still send a shiver down her spine when she recalls the austere strictness of the household. The kitchen was strictly kosher and Kitty was forbidden to touch anything.

Once, she went with her grandmother to see a rabbi about whether it was permissible to eat a chicken that was not quite kosher. The rabbi said, 'No.' They were shown the place where the kosher chickens were slaughtered: a nightmare scene with the stench of death and blood splattered everywhere. Kit haunted by the experience—absolutely distraught for v and weeks. That is all she recalls being taught by her grandmother about being Jewish. Jewishness was just a matter of rules: don't touch this, and don't eat that.

In primary school Kitty failed in just one subject—and that was the Jewish religion. Her father was appalled, and felt a great embarrassment to the family, so he arranged for some coaching for Kitty from the girl next door. Her name was Eva and she was very Jewish. She used to come over and try to teach Kitty to read Hebrew—but without success.

Kitty was sent to a public primary school, and then to Lazar Piroska, a private school mainly for Jews. However, like her parents, this school was not particularly religious or earnest about Jewishness. After four years she moved on to study at the Commercial Academy. It was from there that Kitty had ended up in the private preparatory college in Purkersdorf, run by closet Nazis.

Although the events swirling around them had an impact on millions of lives across Europe, for Kitty it was personal. A settled anger had taken root in her heart focused on one man: the pale, puffy-faced man she had seen from a distance of just six feet—Adolf Hitler.

But for the moment such thoughts were put to one side. Before her was Italy and the Adriatic Sea, and a chance to relax with her family—while there was still time.

They travelled by train to San Martino di Castrozza in the Dolomites, the mountain range in the north east of Italy, and spent two weeks there. There they made friends with a family from Trieste who also had an only child, a daughter close to Kitty's age.

After a fortnight they moved on, again by train, down from the Alps and across the coastal plain to Venice. Here they

Kitty and Ada in Italy, 1939.

Ada and Aladar in Venice, the day the war broke out.

stayed on the Lido at the Hotel de Baine. In the evenings they went to the casino at the Excelsior Hotel.

On the evening of Thursday August 31, 1939, while the Kalafonis were relaxing, in Venice a million and a half German troops were moving forward to their final positions on the Polish border for the invasion that was to begin at dawn the next day.

At daybreak on Friday September 1, 1939, the German armies poured across the Polish frontier and moved towards Warsaw from the north, south and west. German warplanes filled the skies, roaring towards their targets: Polish troops, ammunition dumps, bridges, railways and open cities. Within minutes death and destruction poured from the skies in the infamous *blitzkrieg* technique that became the hallmark of Hitler's war machine.

That morning Kitty and her family were sitting on the sand in the little beach tent provided by the hotel for its guests, with the gentle waves of the Adriatic washing up the beach a few metres from them. A little boy came rushing over gabbling something in Italian that ended with the words 'boom, boom'. He was trying to tell them that a shooting war had begun.

That night the whole of Venice was in darkness as the authorities ordered a complete blackout. Kitty stood on the balcony captivated by the eerie sight of one of the world's most beautiful cities plunged into total darkness. Throughout the hotel guests were hastily packing up and returning to their homes fearing that the German invasion of Poland was about to plunge the whole of Europe into war.

The Kalafonis, however, could not go home, because Budapest's reaction to the German invasion of Poland had been to once again close the borders to all traffic. Kitty's father telephoned the Trieste family they had befriended at San Martino di Castrozza in the Dolomites to explain that they could not get back to their home. Their friends booked the Kalafonis into the Hotel Savoy in Trieste, and Kitty and her parents caught the train around the coast to the western shore of the Gulf of Venice, and waited there in Trieste for the Hungarian borders to be re-opened.

In London, at six minutes past noon on Sunday September 3, 1939, after the failure of 39 hours of desperate negotiations, British Prime Minister Neville Chamberlain stood up in the House of Commons to announce that Britain, along with France, was now at war with Germany.

His words came crackling over BBC radio into the Hotel Savoy in Trieste: 'This is a sad day for all of us, and to none is it sadder than to me. Everything that I have worked for, everything that I have believed in during my public life has crashed into ruins.' Aladar Kalafoni turned to his wife and daughter with anxiety deeply etched in his face. He said, quietly and solemnly, 'it may well be that our lives are about to crash into ruins as well.'

That night, Sunday September 3, 1939, Hitler sent a secret message to Moscow inviting the Russians to join the invasion of Poland.

The Poles were completely overwhelmed by the German onslaught. The terrifying battle technique of *blitzkrieg* was based on speed and firepower: Stuka dive bombers screamed out of the skies, dropped their deadly loads, and wheeled back up into the clouds having spread flames and fear; wave after wave of tanks, whole divisions of them, broke through and thrust forward thirty or forty miles a day; self-propelled, rapid-firing heavy guns rolled at forty miles an hour even down the bumpy, muddy Polish roads; and even the infantry was motorized, arriving in great numbers and at great speed.

On Tuesday September 5, Russia's Foreign Minister, Vyacheslav Mikhailovich Molotov, sent a note to Adolf Hitler accepting his invitation and saying that 'at a suitable time'

Kitty in Venice.

Russian forces would join the attack on Poland.

The Poles never stood a chance. Within the first 48 hours the Polish Air Force was destroyed. Krakow, Poland's second city, fell to the Germans on Wednesday September 6. In one week the Polish Army had been utterly vanquished. The world was stunned by the speed at which the German armies hurtled through Poland.

Finally, the Hungarian government reopened the borders and Kitty and her family were able to catch a train back to their apartment in Budapest. But this journey was very different from the journey with which their holiday had begun. Their journey out had been hopeful and happy. Their return was grim and grey, as all three of them knew that they were travelling deeper into the shadow of the Nazi war machine.

War is not just the story of leaders of armies and of populations—it is the story of families and of individuals who are caught up in its flames. Kitty was just one blonde-haired, 20-year-old Jewish girl, but for her, as for so many others, this war would be a story of deep personal loss. She would be like so many other powerless individuals buffeted by the cyclone of war. When the storm was gone, Kitty would be able to look at the devastation around her and realise how much she had lost. From that loss would grow a deep, sullen resentment that slowly turned into a burning bitterness.

8

AT FIRST EVERYTHING was normal in the Kalafoni household. Aladar went to work each day, the maid cooked and cleaned, Ada socialised, and Kitty met her friends.

Every night Kitty and her parents gathered around the radio to listen to the news. The BBC radio service, crackling through the air by short wave from London, was especially important to them. For a time there was a period of relative quiet, known as 'the phoney war'. But as a bitter winter set in, and the Danube froze, it became clear that before long most of the world would be engulfed in the conflict.

Horthy's Hungarian government did not officially become a combatant in the Second World War until April 10, 1941. But from the beginning it was clear that Hungary was one of the Axis powers, an ally of the new German empire known as the Third Reich.

Hungary seemed to act partly out of approval of German policy and partly out of nervous fear of Hitler's unpredictability and vast military power. As early as July 24, 1939, the Prime Minister of Hungary, Count Teleki, had written identical letters to Hitler and Benito Mussolini, the fascist dictator of Italy, saying that 'in the event of a general conflict Hungary will make her policy conform to the policy of the Axis.' Then he hesitated, apparently fearful of the commitment he had made, and later that same day wrote a second letter stating that 'in order to prevent any possible misinterpretation of my letter of July 24, I...repeat that Hungary could not, on moral grounds, be in a position to take armed action against Poland.'

This hesitation made Hitler furious. On August 8, 1939, Hitler met with Hungary's foreign minister, Count Csáky, in the presence of his own foreign minister Ribbentrop.

'I was shocked,' shouted Hitler, boiling with rage, 'shocked by that letter. I expect no help,' he fumed, pacing back and forth, 'from little Hungary or any other country in my war with Poland. The might of the German war machine will crush Poland.'

Poland, continued the Nazi dictator, posed no problem that the German military could not quickly overcome without help from any other country. However, there was always that possibility that war could start on two fronts—if Britain and France moved quickly to come to Poland's aid.

'No power in the world,' he boasted, 'can penetrate Germany's western fortifications. Nobody,' he continued, his voice rising, 'nobody in all my life has been able to frighten me, and that goes for Britain. Nor will I succumb to the nervous breakdown that some predict. As for Russia—they will never fight against us. They will not repeat the Czar's mistake and bleed to death for Britain. They want to enrich themselves— possibly with the Baltic states—with as little fighting as possible by their own army.'

The Hungarian foreign minister met Hitler again later the same day and was subjected to a second wild tirade along the same lines.

'If the unthinkable were to happen,' shouted the Nazi leader, 'and were Germany ever to be defeated in war, just remember that Hungary would be automatically smashed too.'

It was effective. Count Csáky requested the obsessive dicta- tor 'to regard the two letters written by Teleki as not having been written.'

Hungary was welded tightly to German policy. There was no escaping the alliance. And part of any such alliance was the sup- pression of Jews. No country could be an ally of Hitler that was not prepared to ruthlessly suppress their Jewish population.

During the 'phoney war' period Aladar Kalafoni would meet his Jewish friends in the cafés of Budapest and all the talk would be speculation as to how long it would be before their rights as citizens and Hungarians would be taken away. Not *if* it would happen, but *when* it would happen.

A level of anti-Semitism had always been present in Hungary. Over a decade earlier a law had been passed restricting Jewish entrance to university to 6% (the percentage of Jews in the population). Before this law was passed, up to 30% of university students had been Jewish.

As the months rolled on, the long-feared suppression came. Not all at once, but slowly, step by relentless step. It was like living through a nightmare in slow motion.

Although Great Britain and France had declared war on Germany on September 3, 1939, two days after the invasion of Poland, the two countries stood by while Poland collapsed. France moved troops to the Maginot Line, a belt of steel and concrete fortresses it had built after World War I along its border with Germany. Britain sent a small force into northern France. Germany stationed troops on the Siegfried Line, a strip of defences Hitler built in the 1930s opposite the Maginot Line. The two sides avoided fighting in late 1939 and early 1940.

In April 1940, Hitler invaded Norway. The Nazi *blitzkrieg* military machine moved through Denmark as part of the push into Norway. Britain tried to help its Scandinavian allies, but Germany's powerful *Luftwaffe* had complete control of the air, and prevented all but a handful of British ships and troops from reaching Norway—which fell to the Germans in June 1940.

And over each country conquered by the Germans the terror of the Gestapo was imposed. 'Gestapo' was the name by which the *Geheime Staatspolizei* or Secret State Police force of Nazi

Germany was known. Party officials had first used the Gestapo, noted for its brutality, to smash opposition within the party. Under the brutal direction of Heinrich Himmler the Gestapo used torture and terror to exercise absolute domination over the conquered areas of Europe—and, in particular, to carry out Nazi policy against the Jews.

Neville Chamberlain resigned as British Prime Minister after the invasion of Norway. Winston Churchill moved into 10 Downing Street on May 10, 1940. Speaking to the British people and the House of Commons Churchill said, 'You ask what is our policy—our policy is to wage war.' He told them he had nothing to offer but 'blood, toil, tears, and sweat.'

Belgium, Luxembourg, and the Netherlands had hoped to remain neutral after World War Two began. But Germany launched its mighty *blitzkrieg* machine against them on May 10, 1940. They immediately requested help. Luxembourg surrendered in one day, and the Netherlands in five. British and French forces rushed into Belgium and into the jaws of a trap. As they raced northwards, the main German invasion force cut behind them through the Belgian Ardennes Forest in the south. The Germans reached the English Channel on May 21. By then they almost surrounded the Allied forces.

King Leopold III of Belgium surrendered on May 28, 1940. His surrender left the British and French forces still trapped in Belgium in great danger. They were retreating towards the French seaport of Dunkirk. Britain sent all available craft to rescue the troops. The rescue fleet included destroyers, yachts, ferries, fishing boats and tugboats. Under heavy bombardment, the vessels evacuated 338,000 troops from May 26 to June 4. The evacuation of Dunkirk saved most of Britain's army, but left behind were all the tanks, heavy weapons and equipment. The remaining Allied troops in Dunkirk surrendered on June 4, 1940.

That same day Winston Churchill rose
Parliament to say. 'Even though large tracts
fallen, or may fall, into the grip of the Gestapo
ous apparatus of Nazi rule, we shall go on to th
fight in France, we shall fight in the seas and oceans, we shall
fight with growing confidence and growing strength in the
air—we shall defend our island, whatever the cost may be. We
shall fight on the beaches, we shall fight on the landing
grounds, we shall fight in the fields and in the streets, we shall
fight in the hills. We shall never surrender.'

Meanwhile, France was expecting a replay of the First World
War—a battle along a stationary front, which was why the
Maginot Line had been built. But German tanks and aircraft
swept around the defensive line. The major assault against
France was launched on June 5. The French forces reeled backwards under the powerful onslaught of the *blitzkrieg*. As France
collapsed, Italy joined the war as Germany's ally on June 10.

German troops entered Paris on June 14, 1940.

Hitler was convinced that Britain would seek peace with
Germany after the fall of France. But Britain fought on alone.
Hitler made preparations to cross the English Channel with an
invasion force. Before the Germans could invade, however, they
had to defeat the Royal Air Force. This conflict became known
as the Battle of Britain. Intense German bombing raids known
as the Blitz took place nearly every night over London throughout the autumn and winter of 1940-41.

All this time the Hungarian authorities were keeping a nervous eye on their German masters.

In August 1940 an official letter arrived by post informing
Aladar Kalafoni that he had been called up to serve in a compulsory labour unit. The letter informed him when and where
he was to report for duty. The next day he told his employers

ʌhe notice he had received.

At that time Hungary was the world's leading exporter of goose feathers, for use in pillows and bedding. Aladar Kalafoni was chief accountant with the largest syndicate involved in the goose feather export trade. His cousins in New York were part of this booming trade—they imported goose feathers for the whole of North America.

On being shown the letter his employers told him the call-up was unavoidable, and there was nothing they could do about it, but they would keep his job open for him, and he could come back to it when his period of forced labour was over.

Kitty was furious about what was happening to her father.

'Slave labour, Papa,' she said. 'That's what they are forcing you to do—slave labour.'

Those being called up into forced labour units were Jewish males who were physically fit. This call-up was part of a series of "Jewish Rules" that were to make life increasingly unbearable for Jews in Hungary.

Aladar was made part of a road mending gang. Each member of the labour unit was made to wear a white skullcap to show that they were Jews working under the compulsory labour laws. He was sent to a remote rural part of Hungary and Ada and Kitty did not see their husband and father for months.

Eventually the six months of his call-up period expired, Aladar returned home, and returned to his old job. But not for long. Within a year the newspapers were full of what they called the next "Jewish Rule." This said that no Jew was allowed to hold a senior or important position. Clearly this included Aladar Kalafoni as chief accountant of an important export industry. Once again his employers, who were also relatives, were unable to protect him—and he lost his job.

Then came the second letter, calling him back to forced labour on the roads. This time it was not for a fixed period, but for as

Aladar on the first day of forced labour.

long as the authorities wanted to keep him. Overnight this "Jewish Rule" reduced Kitty's father from distinguished professional to slave labourer.

Over the long months that followed, Kitty and her mother saw Aladar only briefly, when he was allowed to visit for a day or two. The rest of the time he was working in a road gang—digging ditches and shovelling gravel—in some remote border area: one month near Slovakia, the next on the Ukrainian border. They knew what he was doing, and what he was living through, mainly from his letters.

In 1942 a letter arrived telling them that he had been gravely ill. Kitty and her mother were worried and anxious, but at first there was little they could do. The next letter informed them that the illness had been due to tonsillitis, and his tonsils had been removed by a doctor in a small town on the Ukrainian border. Kitty's mother, Ada, was allowed to travel to where he was posted in order to nurse him back to health. But he was given the minimum time to recover, and then compelled to return to the road gang. Ada returned to Budapest, and to the apartment that she shared with Kitty and the young maid who still worked for them (in wartime Hungary there was nowhere else for the maid to go).

Hitler used threats to force Hungary (along with Bulgaria and Romania) into joining the Axis. All three countries supplied Germany with food, petrol and other vital supplies. And before long Hungarian troops were fighting alongside German soldiers.

With this support in place Hitler began planning his long contemplated invasion of Russia. However, he was delayed by the need to rush his forces to the aid of his major ally, Italy, whose army was doing badly in the battle to conquer Greece. And then the armed forces of Yugoslavia rebelled and overthrew their own government, which had signed an agreement with the Axis in

March 1941. A furious Adolf Hitler ordered that Yugoslavia be crushed. The German assault began on April 6—and was all over in 11 days.

The detours into Yugoslavia and Greece were costly for Hitler because they delayed his invasion of the Soviet Union. Hitler confidently predicted victory over the Soviet Union within eight weeks, but the delay meant that he was now facing the deadly Russian winter.

For Kitty and her mother things were becoming more difficult. There were food shortages and rationing, and the absence of Aladar's salary made their situation financially precarious (he received no wages for his forced labour). For a time they drew on their savings, and then they began to sell small items of jewellery. Kitty remembers a gold necklace that was sold one link at a time to buy food. And, to make matters worse, there was now a powerful Hungarian Nazi Party called the *Nyilas* (or Arrow-Cross) looking for opportunities to terrorise and suppress Hungary's Jewish population.

On top of which there were now large numbers of German troops in Hungary, which was being used by Hitler as a staging post for "Operation Barbarossa"—his invasion of the Soviet Union. This massive operation finally began on June 22, 1941.

As a result, the RAF began to bomb Budapest—sporadically at first, but building in intensity over the next two years.

Soviet forces held off the German advance along a massive front in eastern Europe in 1942 and won a major victory at Stalingrad in 1943. The Allies invaded northern Africa in 1942 and forced Italy to surrender in 1943. The tide of war was now flowing in a new direction—against Hitler and his Nazi thugs.

By 1943 Hitler had ceased to regard Hungary as a reliable ally. By early 1944 it was becoming clear that Germany was losing the war. World War II was now entering its final phase: a phase that would end with the death of Hitler and the liberation of Western

Europe. In these closing bloody weeks Hitler knew that all was lost and his actions were now driven by implacable genocidal fury.

The war to build a great German empire had failed, but the war against the Jews would be fought to the last minute, and the last bullet. He took aim at the only remaining large Jewish population in Europe: the Jews of Hungary. German forces invaded Hungary on March 19, 1944. Before the year was out 440,000 Hungarian Jews would die.

9

MARCH 19, 1944 WAS a Friday, a cool, brisk Spring day
with no sign, as yet, of the Summer that was coming. It was "St
Joseph's Day" in Hungary, where the tradition was to celebrate
with a party on your "name day"—the day of the saint after
whom you had been named. On this particular March 19th
Kitty's father was home with his family, having been given a few
days leave from his forced labour camp. One of his best friends
was Joseph Benes—the general manager of Hungary's largest
chemical factory. The Benes family lived on the outskirts of
Budapest. They had a country house, and a small hobby farm, in
an exclusive area at the village of Leanyfolu. Aladar and Ada
Kalafoni took a train out to Leanyfolu to celebrate St Joseph's
Day with the Benes family—leaving Kitty alone in the apartment
with the maid.

In the middle of the afternoon Kitty walked out onto her balcony on the east side of the Danube river. At first she noticed
nothing but the cool, crisp weather and the wintry sunlight glint-
ing on the water. Then she looked at the west bank—and could-
n't believe her eyes. There were tanks on the road that ran
beside the river over there, wave after wave of tanks, armed per-
sonnel carriers, troop transports, sleek officers' cars, and self-
propelled heavy guns. It was an army on the move—a huge,
heavily equipped army. And on every vehicle, and every piece of
ordinance, was the red and black Nazi insignia.

Kitty called to the maid to come and see.

'What's going on?' asked the frightened girl. 'What does it
mean?'

'I don't know,' replied Kitty slowly. 'I'm not sure.' But after a
moment's thought she was sure. This could mean only one thing.

'The Germans have invaded,' said Kitty quietly, unaware that she had spoken aloud.

The maid gave a squeal of terror, and then placed her hand over her mouth to stop the sound, as if afraid that she might be heard by the advancing soldiers far away across the broad Danube.

The parade of military vehicles and weapons went on and on. The two women stood there, transfixed, unbelieving, watching what was happening for a very long time.

At last they went inside and Kitty turned on the radio, wanting to hear the news. The radio was playing music, and she had to wait a long time for a news bulletin. Eventually it came, and the news reader announced that the Germans were arriving in response to an 'invitation' from the government of the Hungarian Regent, Admiral Miklos Horthy.

The truth that only slowly became apparent over the next twelve weeks was that Hitler, in the final phase of World War II, was determined to pursue his war against the Jews. It was Berlin that had informed Horthy that he was 'inviting' them in—with the support of the local *Nyilas* party.

Kitty clicked off the radio, and walked back out on to the balcony. Still the endless parade of advancing German military might was moving down the road on the western side of the Danube. Soon German soldiers, and military vehicles, seemed to be in every street in Budapest. Kitty's first concern was for her parents. Would they be able to get back home from Leanyfalu with this German military presence everywhere?

'What will happen?' asked the maid, with a note of panic in her voice. 'Will they come here?'

'I don't know,' Kitty responded, her anxiety almost matching that of the maid. 'I have no idea what will happen, or what they will do.'

It was late that night when the front door of the apartment

opened, and Kitty's parents stepped in. Kitty thre
her father's arms.

'Papa, oh Papa. I didn't know if you would b
back—or if I would ever see you again.'

'It took us ages,' her father explained. 'We set out as soon as
we heard the news. One of Joseph's neighbours rushed in to tell
us, and then we turned on the radio and heard for ourselves. We
were worried about you Kitty, so we set out at once. But there
are soldiers and checkpoints all over the city, and it took us
ages.'

This was the second time Kitty had observed a German invasion, first in Austria and now in Hungary—both in response to
a so-called 'invitation'. The Hungarians, she noticed, were not
quite like the Austrians. Some people were happy to see the
Germans come—the Nazi members and sympathisers—but many
people were nervous about the presence of so many German
soldiers not only on Hungarian soil, but in charge of the day to
day administration of Hungary. And now people knew much
more about the Nazis than had been the case in Austria in 1939.
Nazi rule meant the SS and the Gestapo and the loss of freedom
for everyone.

There was also a very large Jewish population, and the Jews
were as much Hungarian as Jewish—popular members of the
community with many non-Jewish friends and roots deep in the
Hungarian soil. And everyone knew what the presence of Nazi
troops would mean for the Jews.

The German occupation meant that the allied bombing of
Budapest increased. From April 2 the bombing went on relent-
lessly, both day and night. The US Air Force Flying Fortress
bombers roared overhead by daylight, flying from bases in Italy
and dropping their deadly payloads. At night they were
replaced by RAF Lancasters.

Kitty and Ada kept a small bag packed with a few essentials by the door of their apartment, and when the sirens sounded they, and the other inhabitants of their apartment block, scrambled down to the basement air raid shelter to wait for the bombing to stop.

10

IN THE TWELVE WEEKS following the German invasion everything changed for Hungarian Jews. First, they were ordered to wear the yellow star of David on their clothes whenever they went out in public.

Aladar Kalafoni, and the other Jewish men in the forced labour units, were ordered back to Budapest where a school was turned into a barracks to house them. They didn't know at the time that this move was just to make it easier for the Germans to ship them off to the death camps. With her father back in the city Kitty, courageously or foolishly, would remove the yellow star from her clothes and sneak out to visit him from time to time at the school where he was confined. She always took him a little of their precious food.

The last time Kitty went to see her father she found the school building deserted. One old man was sweeping out the central quadrangle, so Kitty approached him.

'Where is everyone? Just yesterday this place was crowded. I came to visit my f...' her voice trailed away, uncertain how much it was safe to reveal.

The old man didn't stop sweeping. 'All marched out this morning,' he said without looking up. 'Straight after breakfast they were rounded up and marched off.'

'Marched off where? Where did they go to?'

'The trains. They're probably half way to Germany by now.' Then he stopped and laughed bitterly, 'or, knowing how the trains run these days, they're still at the station waiting for the line to clear.'

'At the station,' gasped Kitty. 'Thank you...thank you...'

'I just said "might be",' he called after her, but Kitty was paying no attention.

She knew where the trains for Germany carrying prisoners and Jews left from—the main railway station on the outskirts of Budapest. Kitty caught a tram to the railway station.

As she hurried up onto the platform she was ignored by the young men in uniform. They were all too busy to pay attention to a lone, young woman. She was in such a hurry, and so intent on what she was doing, Kitty may well have looked to them as if she had business at the station—a legitimate reason for being there. Perhaps they took her for a secretary sent to the station to hand deliver a message. For whatever reason, they paid no attention.

Breathlessly she asked a platform attendant, 'Have any trains left this morning for Germany?'

'This morning? No, none so far. We're expecting the signal soon, so...'

She didn't hear the rest, she was hurrying down the platform. There she found a long train comprising entirely of cattle trucks—each wagon packed full of human beings: Jewish men.

Hands, bodies and faces could be seen through the wooden slats in the railway wagons. For several hours Kitty walked up and down the platform hoping to see her father.

Despite the German guards on patrol at the railway station no one stopped her or asked what she was doing. She had made up her mind that if she was stopped she would explain that her father was somewhere on the train, and, as far as she was concerned, they might as well ship her off with him—wherever he was going.

But no one took any notice of her.

Kitty walked the length of that platform, back and forth, peering at the crowded cattle wagons. At each wagon she would stop and search silently, wondering, 'Papa! Papa! Can you see me?'

CHAPTER 10

Pale desperate faces looked back at her—but not her father's face.

She was so close to the cattle wagons that some of the hands reaching out through the slatted slides tried to grab her, to touch her.

'Tell my wife...tell my wife...' one hoarse voice cried out at her. Kitty was paying no attention. It was her own father she was desperate to see. It was his voice she was dying to hear.

An hour passed, and then a second. Still she searched.

'Papa! Papa! Can you see me?' she whispered.

Still she found no sign. Her father must be jammed in the middle of one of those packed wagons, unable to move, unable to call out. Perhaps he was on the far side of one of the trucks. Perhaps he was squashed in a corner in an overcrowded cattle wagon.

'Papa! Papa! Can you see me?' she screamed silently to herself.

From one end of the platform to the other, and then back again.

'Papa! Papa!'

Finally, at the end of the platform a signal changed and with a hiss of steam and a clank of metal the locomotive began to move. Slowly at first, and then gathering speed.

As the final car on the train passed her Kitty called out one last time: 'Papa! Papa!'

Kitty never saw her father or heard his voice that day, although she hoped that perhaps he had caught a glimpse of her. Yes, she told herself, perhaps he had. It was a hope that lived with her for a long time.

Finally the last car of the train rattled over the points, around a curve in the line, and disappeared in the distance.

Unbeknown to Kitty that train took her father to Auschwitz Concentration Camp.

II

THE SS AND GESTAPO ordered the remaining Jews in Budapest to live in designated apartment blocks. If an apartment block had more Jewish than non-Jewish residents it was designated a "Jewish building" and a large yellow star was painted on the front door. However, if the reverse was the case it was designated a gentile building and Jews were forbidden to live there: instead, they had to move into one of the designated Jewish buildings.

The apartment block where Kitty and her mother lived was a designated Jewish building, and soon they found their small apartment housing themselves and several other displaced Jewish families as well.

The first thing the authorities did with the Jewish houses was to collect the radios. No one living in a Jewish house was allowed to have a radio. Everyone obeyed the rule and handed over their radio sets. No one was prepared to try to hide a radio for fear that they would be reported to the authorities.

Next the officials demanded that all Jews hand over their jewellery. This rule was only ever partly observed. Everyone kept something back. But some things could not be kept back. Every married woman was expected to hand over her wedding ring—and this could not be hidden since the authorities knew that every married woman had, if nothing else, a wedding ring. Kitty's mother handed over her wedding ring, and some of their other pieces of jewellery, but they kept back the best pieces, along with the family silver and some other items of value. These they gave to their non-Jewish friends for safe keeping. Not all of these things came back when the war was over.

Under the new rules Jews were only allowed to leave their

designated building between one o'clock and two
afternoon to buy food. Kitty gave her pet fox terr
to a non-Jewish friend, because she could no long
for his necessary daily walk. The building was k . .ʋ⌐⌐ea,
except between one and two, and the janitor, a non-Jew, was in
charge of the house.

Because Kitty had many gentile friends, she would quite
often remove the yellow star from her clothes and sneak out of
the building at all hours of the day—much to her mother's
alarm. This was possible because the janitor had a daughter
about Kitty's age, and the two were friends. She would unlock
the front door to let Kitty out, and then, when she returned let
her back in again.

On one occasion there was a non-Jewish man, a film pro-
ducer named Gaza Bolgár, who was fond of Kitty and wanted
to see her, so he arrived at this "Jewish house" with two gypsy
musicians he had hired. He had them play as loudly as they
could under Kitty's balcony. Then he went to the janitor and
said he wanted to take his girlfriend out. The janitor—perhaps
irritated by the loud gypsy music—relented, and allowed Kitty
to go out.

In the summer of 1944 Kitty was directed to work in the
Gadanyi factory packing sterilised bandages to be sent to the
front-line. Many of the trams had stopped running because of
the war conditions, and Kitty had to walk the long distance to
and from work. But, for eight hours each day, it got her out of
the building that had become a prison, and out of the crowded
apartment that now held 20 people as well as Kitty and her
mother. And each day she had to carry the official permit that
said she was allowed out of her "Jewish house" to do slave
labour.

Now, when the sirens sounded and the bombs started

ling, the basement of the apartment block was packed with people.

In October it all changed again. The Nazi rulers of Hungary announced that from now on all Jewish men and women over the age of 50 would have to move into a newly created ghetto— the apartment buildings that had been designated Jewish houses were now being requisitioned by the government to house soldiers. (All the Jewish men under 50 had already been shipped off to the death camps by this time.)

Dohany Street, in the overcrowded part of Budapest, had been closed off with barbed wire, and this block was now designated the 'Jewish ghetto'. The area fenced off for the ghetto was not large, and it was obvious that once the remaining population of Jewish women moved in there it would be dreadfully overcrowded. Kitty's mother was not quite old enough to qualify, but the anxieties of the war years had aged her, and she could pass as 50. Moving into the ghetto was the only option.

At the same time, all Jewish women under 50 were given different orders.

What these orders were became apparent when the janitor of their apartment block knocked on their front door early one morning.

Kitty's mother answered the door and was brusquely told to fetch her daughter at once.

'Miss Kalafoni,' said the janitor, in the sneering tone that it was now common to adopt when addressing Jews, 'you are to get your things together and wait in the lobby of this building with the rest of the younger women.'

With these words he turned to go.

'Get what things together?' called Kitty after him. 'What shall I need? Where am I going?'

He stopped at the head of the stairs, turned and said, 'you'll need walking shoes, a rucksack carrying basic clothing, and three days food.'

Once more he turned to go.

'Wait,' Kitty called out. 'Where am I going?'

'All of you younger women will go to the Budapest sports ground. That's where you're to assemble. After that...I don't know.'

With those words he was gone.

Kitty slowly closed their apartment door, a thoughtful look on her face.

'I'm not going,' Kitty announced to her mother.

'You're what?'

'I'm not going!'

'Then what will you do?'

'I don't know...I don't know...' muttered Kitty as she paced back and forth.

'But you have no choice, Kitty dear. If they say "go" we have to go.'

'No! No, I won't have it. We're just allowing ourselves to be carted off. I am not a cow to be sent to the slaughterhouse.'

'I'm sure that's not what's happening. It will just be some camp, some ghetto, they will put us in. It won't be nice, but we'll survive.'

There was a bitterness in Kitty's voice as she said, 'I don't trust them, and I don't believe them...and I'm definitely not going!'

'Then what? What will you do? You're being foolish, Kitty.'

'No, mother. I know what I'm doing. Trust me.'

'But what *are* you doing? Where will you go? They've already taken your father, and they're about to send me and the older women off to a ghetto. It's not safe to disobey them. If you do what you're told you just might live. If you disobey them, you'll be dead—and what good will that be?'

Kitty clenched her fists and said firmly, 'I'm not a sheep,

'ying orders. I'm not going.'

ask you again, Kitty dear—where will you go? What
o?'

'I know! I've just remembered. Our friend Feri Skergula told me that I could use his apartment if I needed to. Well, I need to now. He doesn't need it—he's off somewhere with the Hungarian Army. Probably at the Russian front by now. He gave me the key when he left Budapest. I'll take the yellow star off all my clothes and move into his apartment. I'm going into hiding. I'll pass as a gentile.'

'You'll pretend to be *goy*?'

'I'll just mix in and disappear in the crowds.'

'Oh, Kitty darling, is it safe?' asked Ada, wringing her hands in anguish.

'Mama, nothing's safe. But I refuse to surrender to be put into one of those cattle trains and deported somewhere.'

'But if they catch you...?'

'Then they'll ship me out anyway. We don't know where all our relatives have been sent, or what they're facing—but it can't be any worse staying here and taking my chances.'

'But you *have* to go to the sports ground, Kitty darling—you *have* to, or they'll kill you.'

'They might kill me eventually, Mama, but I'm not going to make it easy for them.'

What Kitty didn't say out loud was how much she hated these Nazi overlords, and how she was determined to make things as difficult as possible for those she hated so bitterly. If they wanted her, well, they would have to find her.

12

IT WAS A COLD OCTOBER afternoon when Kitty and her mother left their apartment for the last time in 1944. Ada Kalafoni was going first to another designated "Jewish House" several streets away in the same suburb, at 38 Pozsonyi Street, and from there she would eventually be moved into the Jewish ghetto—and Kitty was about to take up her new life, in hiding.

Ada's new accommodation was classified as a "Vatican protected" Jewish House—a sign to this effect being posted beside the yellow star on the front of the building. At that time in Budapest the only safe Jewish houses were either "Vatican protected" (under the diplomatic protection of the Primate of Hungary, Cardinal Serédy), or else "Swedish protected" (having been established by Raoul Wallenberg, a Swedish businessman and diplomat, who helped save some 100,000 Hungarian Jews from being killed by the Nazis—he often risked his life, and later won worldwide admiration for his heroic efforts). Ada qualified for a "Vatican protected" house because the Kalafonis had officially converted to Catholicism at the outbreak of the war. (The Nazis refused to recognise such conversions, and insisted that such persons were still Jewish, but at least it brought Ada under the protection of the Hungarian Roman Catholic Church.)

Before they left, Kitty packed a suitcase. As well as a selection of such warm, winter clothes as could fit in one bag, she also packed whatever food was left in their apartment. It was not much: dried beans, lentils, a bit of rice and a few cans of tinned food. She packed her thick, warm eiderdown into a carry-bag, together with a small iron cash box.

In 1939 Kitty's father had withdrawn all of the family's savings from the bank, for fear they would eventually fall into the hands of the Nazis. Most of these funds he had sent to his cousin Leslie Ronai in New York to be lodged in a Swiss bank account. The funds that remained (after their Italian holiday had been paid for) were kept in a locked iron cash box—and it was from these funds that the family lived throughout the war. The cash box contained a strange mixtures of currencies: there was Hungarian money (increasingly devalued as the war dragged on), American dollars (sent over by the cousins in New York), and some French gold coins (called "napoleons" because they bore the image of Napoleon I, originally each worth 20 francs but constantly increasing in value because of their high gold content).

Kitty also put a few personal items into her handbag, and cut the yellow star off every item of clothing she owned.

They left when the door of their apartment was unlocked at one o'clock. Kitty held her bag up high so the janitor would not notice there was no yellow star on her coat. Once out in the street Kitty and Ada hugged and kissed goodbye. Then Ada turned around and began walking the few blocks to her new, temporary, accommodation. Kitty watched her for a long time, as her figure got smaller in the distance. She kept watching until Ada turned a corner and disappeared from view. Then Kitty set off in the opposite direction to start her new life—as a Jew in hiding.

She was wearing ski pants and ski boots under her coat to keep out the bitter October winds. As she walked down city streets and across open city squares she looked around. There were armed soldiers and police patrols throughout the city. Was anyone watching her? Was anyone looking at her suspiciously? She had been out without her compulsory star before, but this was different—this time it was permanent.

The city was a shadow of its former self. It had been a beautiful city, a centre of art and high culture. Now it was a city in ruins. Buildings everywhere had been burned out or reduced to rubble by the constant bombing raids. Electricity was only sporadically available. The trams had stopped running entirely.

No one stopped her. No one even looked suspiciously at her. Perhaps the cold weather helped. People everywhere had their collars turned up, and their heads bowed against the wind.

As she got closer Kitty passed one of the bridges over the Danube, and then the Ritz Hotel, the first of a row of hotels that stood on the banks of the river. She came to Vigadó Square. One side of the square was open to the city traffic; on another side stood the elegant Vigadó concert hall; and on the third side was the private house containing the apartment of her absent friend Feri. Beyond the square the line of hotels continued—first the Hungaria Hotel, then the Bristol followed by the Carlton. Beyond the Carlton was a plaza and a grand and beautiful old church.

Feri Skergula had been a solicitor before he was called up into the army. His apartment, he had warned her, was a modest bachelor flat.

The wind that blew between the buildings carried icy mist from the Danube and was bitterly cold. Kitty kept her head down and hurried on. At last she arrived at number 3 Vigadó Square. It was a beautiful building, the only apartment block among a row of elegant hotels. On the ground floor of the apartment building was a coffee shop (in fact, there were coffee shops on the ground floors of many of these buildings).

Her heart sank as she saw, standing beside the entrance steps to the building, two armed and uniformed members of the *Nyilas* with their armbands showing the crossed arrow symbol. But she had come too far, and it was too late now, to turn back.

Kitty kept walking with as much confidence as she could muster. As she passed the armed guards she nodded to them politely, and even managed to smile at them. They smiled back at the pretty young woman, one of them even touched his cap to her, but they said nothing and asked to see no papers.

With a sigh of relief Kitty hurried inside the building and climbed one flight of stairs to Feri's apartment on the first floor. With frozen fingers inside thick gloves she fumbled with the key. Finally, the door swung open, she stepped inside, closed the door and locked it immediately. She put down her bag and leaned back against the closed door to catch her breath. Her heart was pounding. She had made it. She had reached her hiding place.

She was standing in the small entrance hall of the flat. It was cold and dark and smelled of dust. Feri had been in the Hungarian army for over a year, and the last time he had managed to visit to his flat had been over six months earlier.

Kitty tried the light switch. There was no electricity.

'Perhaps Feri never paid his bill,' she said to herself. She spoke out loud, just to hear a human voice in that cold, quiet, dead apartment—any voice, even her own.

'Yes, that's probably it,' she said as she moved cautiously forward. 'I'll bet they sent the electricity bill here after the army had shipped poor Feri out somewhere horrible. Maybe his mail was forwarded to him. Perhaps it never reached it. Or perhaps it did! What fun that would be for poor Feri—to be shivering in the trenches on the Russian front, and open his mail only to find an electricity bill!' Kitty laughed out loud at the foolishness of her own imagination. But suddenly she stopped as a thought hit her.

'Or perhaps he's dead. Maybe his electricity bill is sitting with his army papers, waiting for the war to end.' Thinking of Feri dead brought hot tears to her eyes, and she had to start moving again to drive such images out of her head.

Kitty tried the inner door, and stepped from the entrance lobby of the flat into the main living area. It was a shambles. All the windows had been blown out by the Allied bombing. There were fragments of shattered glass on the window sills and the carpets, and there was dust and grime everywhere.

And it was bitterly cold. One floor below those windows was the promenade, or corso—the broad pedestrian area that ran along the bank of the river. Beyond that was wide, icy expanse of the Danube itself—from where this bone-chilling wind was blowing.

On Kitty's right were three doors leading to a bedroom, a bathroom and a kitchen respectively. As Feri had warned her, even if the apartment had been intact, it was a sparsely furnished and somewhat spartan bachelor dwelling. Kitty walked around and explored the small flat. The bedroom also had windows looking out over the river, and these windows too had been shattered by the bombing. A grey and grimy dust covered everything in the bedroom, and the same icy wind made the room arctic.

The kitchen and bathroom were cleaner, and, Kitty was pleased to discover, the water was still running and gas was still connected. She tried all the light switches and power points but it was just as she had feared—all the electricity to the flat was cut off. In the kitchen Kitty searched for food. There was still salt in the salt shaker, and she found some sugar—but there was no other food in any of the cupboards.

'At least', she thought, 'I'll have some sugar to have with my planter tea.' Planter tea was a herbal tea substitute being used in Budapest at the time, as real tea had been impossible to obtain since the outbreak of the war.

She spent an hour cleaning up as best she could. She cleared away the broken glass and cleaned up the worst of the dust and grime. Then she stood in the bedroom and surveyed her handiwork. Clearly it would be impossible to sleep here, with gaping holes where the windows should be. She stripped off the bedclothes and dragged the mattress out into the small entrance lobby. Here she could, at least, shut the inner door against the night wind, and, if she was rugged up with her eiderdown, she just might manage to sleep.

In the lounge room Kitty found some candlesticks. Then in the kitchen she came across candles and matches. In the windowless entrance lobby it would be safe to light these candles despite the blackout laws, made necessary by the constant bombing raids. At least, she thought, I'll have some light after sunset.

It was now late in the afternoon and already getting dark. Kitty washed up some saucepans, crockery and cutlery, and ate a modest evening meal of hot beans and rice.

Just as she was stacking her plate and saucepan in the sink she heard the first air raid warning of the night. As the siren howled she had to decide what to do. From the stairs could be heard the hurrying footsteps of the other residents as they descended to the building's basement, used as an air raid shelter, to wait for the "all clear".

Kitty knew she couldn't risk joining them. She was a strange face, not one of the known residents. She couldn't risk questions about who she was or where she came from. Clearly, from now on she would have to spend each bombing raid in the apartment—and simply trust that she might survive whatever happened.

The booming thuds of exploding bombs sent her scurrying into the entrance hall of the flat. Here she closed the inner door, to shut out the cold and reduce the sound of the falling bombs. For a time she leaned against the closed door and listened to the ground shaking rumble of exploding bombs. After a while she lit the candles, and huddled in her eiderdown waiting for the night to end, and hoping the cold and the bombs would go away.

Amazingly, she slept. Perhaps it was sheer exhaustion.

A publicity shot of Adolf Hitler, c 1941

13

THE NEXT MORNING KITTY began the daily routine that she was to follow for more than two months.

Each night she slept under her thick eiderdown in the entrance hall of Feri Skergula's flat. The only light she had came from candles. With water and gas available in the kitchen she could cook meals—mostly of beans and lentils—and she could wash her clothes, and the crockery and cutlery she was using. She could try to keep the apartment clean, despite the dust and grit that drifted in day and night through the non-existent front windows.

Most of each day was spent in the apartment, rugged up against the cold, just trying to stay warm. Feri's spartan bachelor flat contained few books, so there was almost nothing to read, and almost nothing to do. Alone in the apartment, for hours each day, Kitty had nothing to fill her time but her own thoughts. She couldn't just sit there shivering all day, she had to do something.

So, despite the danger, Kitty would go out for several hours each day, just to escape for a while from those few small rooms with their broken windows and gritty carpets and furniture, with more grey soot from bombed and burning buildings constantly drifting in.

She would walk the wide boulevards and city squares of Budapest. She would join the other walkers in Budapest's famous Váci Street. If the air raid siren sounded when she was out Kitty could follow the crowds into the nearest air raid shelter, and wait for the bombing to stop. She felt safe in the anonymity of the crowd, while the air raid shelter back at the apartment building was filled with people who knew each other and didn't know her, and who might ask difficult questions.

Sometimes she would buy a newspaper. Sometimes she would pick up a newspaper someone else had discarded, on a bench in a rubbish bin, and take it back to the apartment to give her something to read to fill the long hours alone. Not that the newspapers were large in those wartime conditions—just a few pages. Still, it was something to read.

Sometimes fresh bread was available, and Kitty would use a little of her remaining cash to buy a small loaf, and so vary her plain and limited diet. Sometimes, she would go into one of the many coffee shops of Budapest, to get out of the cold, to buy a cheap cup of coffee, and—if she was feeling reckless—to buy a pastry to eat. Even the most famous coffee shops in Budapest— the Belvárosi, Stühmer's and the Gerbeaud—were struggling to stay open. They were hit just as hard as everyone else by the food shortages, and the war-time food rationing, and the rich cakes and pastries of pre-war Budapest had long since disappeared. But occasionally they would have plain pastries for sale—which were eagerly snapped up by the customers.

Then there was the black market. Everywhere there were people eager to offer deals. One day Kitty was sitting alone, drinking coffee, when a strange man pulled out a chair and took a seat at her table. At first he made casual conversation while looking at her warily, as if sizing her up.

Finally he said, 'You need documents?'

Kitty blinked uncomprehendingly.

'If you need documents, I can sell you documents.'

'A complete set?'

'I don't have complete sets of documents. And anyway, only the very rich can afford them. But I can sell you a blank birth certificate—fill it in yourself, anyhow you wish.'

'How much?'

For some time they haggled over a price, finally agreeing on ten American dollars.

'They must be American dollars, mind,' the man insisted. Having settled the price they agreed to meet at the same place the next day.

They met as arranged and the man led Kitty to a quiet corner. He showed her the blank birth certificate—it certainly looked genuine. Kitty handed over two American five dollar bills, taken that morning from her rapidly dwindling cash box.

Back at the apartment Kitty filled in the blank form, trying to imitate the formal handwriting used by the clerks in government offices. She chose the name "Katalin Kovacs" for herself. Under "religion" she wrote "Roman Catholic". She knew it was not enough by itself. In fact, unless she obtained the other official documents that all citizens were meant to carry at all times she would not dare to produce this one—but this was a start.

Sometimes, as she walked the streets and squares, Kitty would find someone she knew. Some of these were Jews being sheltered by Raoul Wallenberg. He had issued Swedish passports to about 20,000 Jews, allowing them to claim the protection of the neutral Swedish government. He also sheltered Jews in houses he bought or rented with his own money or money from the World Jewish Congress and the American War Refugee Board. Wallenberg, a Lutheran, was assisted by Roman Catholic and other non-Jewish leaders in his rescue efforts.

On one such occasion Kitty ran into her Aunt Jenny, Ada's sister, and Jenny's husband Paul. Jenny and Paul were also Jews in hiding.

'I've seen your mother,' said Uncle Paul.

Kitty was surprised and pleased. She asked whether her mother was well and how she was coping,

'She's well,' replied Paul vaguely. 'She's doing okay.

And then Kitty asked her uncle how he had happened to visit Ada.

'The *Nyilas* were searching for Jews in the area where we're hiding. A man of my age arouses their suspicions at once. I thought Jenny would be safer for a while if I wasn't there, so I went to visit your mother—I'd heard she was staying in a Jewish house in Pozsonyi Street.'

'But they almost caught him there,' said Jenny breathlessly.

Paul explained, 'I was in the apartment that your mother is sharing with a lot of other women when there was a heavy pounding on the door—it was a raid. At Ada's suggestion I climbed into the bed and pulled the covers up around me. The women heaped some clothes and blankets on top of the bed, and sat around the edge of the bed. The *Nyilas* guards stormed through the place, looked at everyone's papers, and never searched the bed! So here I am!'

'And where are you staying?' asked Jenny.

'Are you in hiding too?' Paul wanted to know, dropping his voice to little more than a whisper, just in case someone might hear them.

In response to their questions Kitty told them about Feri's apartment.

For a long moment Uncle Paul and Aunt Jenny looked at each other. Clearly the same thought had occurred to both of them. Jenny hesitated, and so Paul urged her, 'Ask. Kitty can say no if she wants to. Ask her. It can't hurt to ask.'

'Ask what?' Kitty inquired, puzzled.

'Well,' said Aunt Jenny reluctantly, 'it's like this. The place where we're staying is very cramped. Very little room. And there's no electrical power. And it's freezing cold. Paul and I have been looking for somewhere else to move to, and we thought...well, if you don't mind that is...and if there's a spare room where you are...might we...can we move in with you?'

'Yes, of course,' replied Kitty. 'If you really want to. But the place is very small, and very cold—all the windows are broken.

I'm sleeping in the little entrance hall of the flat, but you can try the bedroom if you like.'

They went to a coffee shop to celebrate with warming cups of hot coffee, and then Jenny and Paul Kalotai came back to the apartment with Kitty and she showed them around. On seeing it their faces fell—it was really no better than their present hiding place. But they decided to try it for one night. Kitty and Jenny cleaned up the bedroom and made up the bed.

For Kitty it made a pleasant change to have people to share her meagre food with, and people to keep her company and provide conversation.

When the bombs started to fall that night the three of them sat in the entrance hall around a spluttering candle and talked until it was late and the bombing had stopped. They reminisced about life in Budapest before the war—a life that had been full of parties, good food, good wine and good friends. Uncle Paul became depressed, insisting those days were gone forever.

Eventually the drone of the bombers overhead, and the thud of falling bombs, died away and Paul and Jenny retired to the front bedroom for the night, leaving Kitty to crawl into the cocoon of her eiderdown.

Not long after they had gone to bed the bombers returned in another wave, and the explosions started again.

The next morning Kitty asked them, 'How did you sleep?'

'We didn't!' snapped Paul, looking ashen faced and bleary-eyed.

'It was freezing,' explained Jenny. 'And it was terrifying—being up here on the first floor, under an open window, while the bombs were falling.'

Paul added, 'We couldn't stand it. We're leaving Kitty, you can have this place to yourself.'

'How on earth can you stay here, Kitty?' asked Jenny in a concerned voice. 'It's so cold, and it just isn't safe.'

So Kitty was alone again.

In the bathroom of her bomb-shattered apartment there was a mirror. Standing in front of that mirror one day Kitty made a remarkable discovery.

As she stared at the dishevelled image before her eyes she muttered, 'I'm not afraid.'

It was something she could see in her eyes. There was anger there, a fiery spark—but no fear. She walked back to huddle in her blanket again, away from the shattered windows and the bitter winds, deep in thought.

'What is happening to me? What is all this doing to me?'

She thought back over everything that happened to her since that day in 1938 (it felt like ancient history now) when she had seen Adolf Hitler riding proudly, arrogantly, into Austria. The images of the days and years since then flickered through her mind rapidly.

'Why am I not afraid? Have my feelings died? Can I feel nothing anymore?'

Then a white hot word flashed into her mind, telling her that her feelings were not completely dead: revenge. She realised that part of what was driving her was a determination to live long enough to see these people suffer for what they had done.

Her anger, her bitterness, was a slow, steady fire. It would drive her to take care, to survive, so that when this all ended she would be there to see vengeance fall upon Hitler and the countless thugs who had done his bidding.

14

NOT LONG AFTER HER evening with Aunt Jenny and Uncle Paul, Kitty was walking through the city streets, taking a break from her tiny, uncomfortable living quarters when she came across an old friend—Magda Hirsch, a young woman about the same age as herself. Magda was also a Jew in hiding. They were delighted to see each other again—it was always a pleasure to discover that someone from the old life was still alive and surviving. They hugged, and laughed together, and told each other their stories.

After that first chance encounter they met regularly, and would sometimes go to one of the little coffee houses to warm their hands around hot cups of coffee and talk about old times—those almost forgotten days of peace before the war and the persecution began.

Occasionally Kitty would meet an old gentile friend of hers named Géza Bolgár. When they met Géza would take Kitty to one of Budapest's restaurants that hadn't been bombed out, burned out, or driven out of business. There she would eat a meal that would last her a week—a real feast. Just the memory of it made the beans and lentils taste a little better.

But Kitty remained a Jew in hiding.

Every day she was breaking countless laws: by not carrying identification papers, by not living in the Jewish ghetto, by not wearing the yellow star of David on her clothes. Meetings with Magda and Géza were brief interruptions of happiness in a daily routine dominated by a constant awareness and a caution almost amounting to paranoia. But this was the price Kitty had to pay for staying alive and out of the hands of the authorities.

Alone again in that freezing apartment, she would stare at

her face in the mirror. There was still not a trace of fear. But there was a burning spark of determination: a determination to survive, to see the wicked suffer. That spark was kept alive by a steady, burning flame of quiet anger and bitterness, and by the word that had become her unspoken motto, the word she imagined as a newspaper headline over reports of the trials of Nazi thugs: 'Unforgivable!'

And it was all just a matter of time—just a matter of surviving for long enough, because it had slowly become clear to everyone that the war was ending.

Four months earlier, on the 6th of June, a fleet of thousands of ships had stood off the beaches of Normandy at one o'clock in the morning. As the heavy guns of the big ships launched a murderous assault on the Nazi fortifications on the shore, landing craft carried thousands of young soldiers to the beaches. By that afternoon the Americans had established two beachheads and the British one, and had advanced several miles inland. The liberation of Europe had begun. Hitler now had to fight on two fronts. It gradually became clear that he was losing the war on the western front, and, at the same time, the eastern front was collapsing as the Russian Red Army pushed back the German line.

On September 23rd the Russian Army had entered Hungary, and now they were fighting the retreating Germans, mile by bloody mile, across the Hungarian countryside. The remnant of the Jews of Budapest waited for the Allied advance that would liberate them from fear and oppression.

As the Allied bombing increased, and the advancing Red Army drew closer to Budapest, the fanatical attacks on Jews became more frenzied and vicious. As government control began to break down, self-appointed *Nyilas* gangs invaded Jewish houses (so-called "Yellow Star" houses), and even the headquarters of the Jewish Council. On the day they burst into the offices of the Jewish Council, only one person was in the building, council member Miksa Domonkos. But by pretending to be speaking on the telephone with the government authorities he was able to convince the *Nyilas* to withdraw.

Not everyone was so fortunate.

Nyilas gangs slaughtered Jewish residents at Nepszinhaz Street and Teleki Square. Jewish workers in forced-labour gangs from Obuda were herded to the Danube and shot into the river from Margit Bridge and Chain Bridge. Their favourite execution method was to make three Jews, tied together, stand on the edge of the bridge. Then they would shoot the Jew in the centre of the group at close range. As the dead body fell backwards it would drag the two still living into, and under, the icy water.

A large-scale, unauthorised *Nyilas* action was the herding of a few thousand Jews, including the Chief Rabbi Hevesi, into the synagogues on Rumbach Sebestyen and Dohany Streets. But quick action by diplomats in Budapest representing the neutral states resulted in them being set free the same night—before they could be slaughtered by the trigger-happy Hungarian fascists.

Although these things were not published in the thin, wartime newspapers that were appearing, news of each fresh outrage spread quickly through the grapevine that connected, in a sporadic and uncertain way, the Jews who, like Kitty, were in hiding in gentile buildings.

It was becoming clear to everyone that the war could not go on much longer. As the bombing rumbled on, and the Red Army continued its relentless march on Budapest, all the city's Jews—both those in the ghetto and those in hiding—knew they just had to hang on, to survive a little longer, until the war's end and the defeat of the vicious anti-Semitic fascist forces.

On October 15, 1944, the Hungarian Head of State, Admiral Horthy, went on the air on Radio Budapest calling on the

Hungarian Army to drop their resistance to the advancing Red Army and lay down their arms. The citizens of Hungary were caught by surprise. They were unprepared for such a move and the Army failed to respond to Horthy's call. Within hours of the broadcast, Horthy's orders were countermanded by the Head of the Hungarian General Staff, General Janos Voros.

There was only one radio station in Budapest at the time, and, to prevent a similar action in the future, it was captured by the *Nyilas*. Before long Horthy had fallen and the head of the Arrow-Cross fascist party, Ferenc Szalasi, was propelled into power. In the days that followed Horthy was compelled to sign two documents. In one he retracted his order to the Army, and in the second he transferred power to Ferenc Szalasi. Subsequently, Horthy was taken into so-called "protective German custody" and transported to Bavaria, where he stayed until the end of the war.

The only people pleased by Horthy's announcement were the Jews—those in the ghetto or the "Yellow Star" houses, or those in hiding (like Kitty). For them, the end of resistance to the advancing Russian Army would mean the end of the war and the end of their oppression.

The change of government in Hungary brought new pressure from the Nazi authorities in Berlin to bring about a swift "final solution to the Jewish question."

The notorious war criminal, Adolf Eichmann, was ordered back to Budapest on October 17. Eichmann was a lieutenant colonel in the Nazi secret police, who was later convicted and executed for his part in the killing of some 6 million Jews during World War Two. Eichmann immediately demanded 50,000 more Jewish workers for Hitler's Third Reich and proposed to march them by foot from Budapest to the German border. Thousands died on that gruelling winter march. Hungary was divided into five zones, and with systematic thoroughness,

Eichmann cleared each zone in turn of all the Jews living there—
working from the outer zones inwards, towards Budapest.

As October turned into November Kitty still went out for an
hour or two every day—despite the danger from roaming gangs
of *Nyilas* and German patrols—just to get out of the confines
of the small, lonely, cold apartment in which she was living.
There was no telephone, and, while she was indoors, she had
no communication with anybody. With the electricity off, Feri
Skergula's radio did not work. It was profoundly isolating. And
the cold got worse and worse. By November blocks of ice were
floating down the Danube and the wind that whistled through
the open windows of the apartment felt as if it came directly
from the North Pole.

All the time Kitty's small supply of money in the iron cash
box was dwindling. When she had been living in her apartment,
with her mother, the Benes family (her father's friends) had
been generous with their financial help. And it was the remains
of their gifts of cash, together with the remains of the family
savings, that now sat in Kitty's padlocked iron cash box.

15

EVERY TIME KITTY LEFT the apartment she was risking her life. Looking back years later she was to say, 'I don't know if I was courageous, or just reckless and foolish. At the time I just seemed to be insensitive to the danger.' In part she knew she was driven by sheer hatred of those who oppressed her—and millions of others—and was determined not to let her oppressors get the better of her.

As a result, there were frequent narrow escapes from the heavy hand of the authorities.

Late one afternoon, as it was getting dark, Kitty was crossing one of Budapest's main squares when she was stopped by a police patrol.

'Papers please, miss,' said the officer in charge.

Those words were heard often in Budapest in those terrible closing days of World War Two—'Papers please,' however politely said meant that you had to establish to the authorities that you had a right to be where you were, or face immediate arrest.

'Papers please, miss,' repeated the policeman.

'Just a moment,' said Kitty, opening her handbag, 'I know I have them here somewhere.'

She dug deep into her handbag, pretending to search for identity papers she knew were not there.

'Oh, dear me,' muttered Kitty, putting on the best act she could. 'Don't tell me I've left them at home. I know I'm not supposed to do that, and I try to be so careful to carry them with me all the time.'

'If you can't produce your papers, miss, I'll have to take you back to the police station with me.'

Kitty's heart sank at those words, but
search. Perhaps something would happe
get tired of waiting for her to find her pa
her way?

As her hands moved feverishly throug
handbag they brought to the top a small,
that had been given to her. It was a picture of Stephen Kaszap:
if not officially a saint, Kaszap was, none the less, deeply revered
by all Hungarian Catholics. The picture had been given to her
by her father's friends, Joseph and Irma Benes, who stood as
godparents when Kitty and Mama and Papa had been baptized
into the Roman Catholic church.

Just as Kitty was losing hope the policeman, becoming restless, leaned forward and glanced into her handbag. He immediately saw the picture of Stephen Kaszap.

On seeing the picture he nodded, smiled, and said, 'It's all
right, miss. Just make sure you have your papers next time.'
Then he turned and went on his way.

'Oh, thank you...' said Kitty quietly, to the uniformed back
that was marching away briskly across the square.

As she hurried home to the safety of her apartment Kitty
thought about what had happened—thought, and wondered.
And before she was halfway home the truth struck her: he had
taken the postcard to be proof that she was Roman Catholic,
that she was not a Jew. It was Jews he was looking for, and
Jews, he had thought, would not carry pictures of Stephen
Kaszap.

November turned into December and the weather grew
colder than Kitty had dreamed possible. Snow began falling,
and fewer people were seen on the streets.

Just three days before Christmas Kitty met up with Magda
once more. The two young women stamped their feet and
slapped their sides to warm up, and then, as soft flakes of snow

The life-saving photo of Stephen Kaszap.

began to fall again, they hurried into a warm coffee shop out of the weather.

Seated at a corner table Kitty said, 'What are we going to do to celebrate Christmas?'

'Christmas?'

'Yes, Christmas,' repeated Kitty firmly. 'Even though we are Jewish, Christmas has always been a big celebration in my family. Every year we had a Christmas tree. We always did that—a beautifully decorated Christmas tree. And on Christmas Eve we always had a big family dinner. It was always fish, I remember those dinners so well—always paprika fish. It was a tradition in our family.'

Even as she spoke Kitty realised that she had said 'was' not 'is'. It was her deeply suppressed fear speaking, the fear that her family would never be together again. And that fear was driving the hatred that was filling more and more of her heart.

'Well, I suppose we could do something,' Magda responded.

'Yes, let's,' enthused Kitty, determined not to give in to the sad and bitter thoughts that threatened to engulf her. 'What are you planning to do? Let's get together, and do something together. Come to my place. It's just as safe as where you are. Then at least we'll be together.'

'And we'll try to get some food,' volunteered Magda, becoming enthusiastic, 'some special food—something nice.'

The two girls pooled their slender financial resources and went shopping. There was very little on the shop shelves, and most of what there was they couldn't afford to buy. They managed to buy a tin of raisins, some fresh bread rolls from the bakery, a small piece of meat (purchased on the black market, "under the counter") and a few other small luxuries—including a bottle of real champagne. Then they went to a florist shop. After much hunting around for something they could afford, Kitty finally purchased a tiny, artificial Christmas tree decorated with pink ribbons and pink candles.

'Oh, that looks so pretty,' gushed Magda, as they left the florist shop. 'We really *will* have a celebration—despite everything.'

Christmas Eve came and Kitty cleaned and re-cleaned the little apartment, trying to remove the dust and grit and grime that drifted in every day. And there were drifting snowflakes making everything damp, and making the task so much harder. Eventually she had cleaned and tidied to her satisfaction. She prepared some food in the kitchen and set up the tiny Christmas tree, with its small candles ablaze, to wait for Magda.

An hour passed, and then another. Kitty found herself checking her wristwatch every few minutes. Magda had not come, and Kitty was worried: what could have happened to her? It was impossible not to worry. Another hour passed, and another.

Kitty and Magda both knew the risks that Jews without papers faced every time they crossed the city.

Had Magda run into one of those police patrols? Kitty wondered.

'Papers please, miss.'

And she would have had no papers.

Is that what had happened?

The time slowly dragged towards midnight. Still Magda did not come. Finally, Kitty accepted the inevitable, blew out the candles on the Christmas tree, and prepared to go to bed for the night. Later Kitty learned that the worst had happened: Magda had been arrested that afternoon. She didn't live to see Christmas Day.

In the darkness, Magda Hirsch had been taken by a *Nyilas* gang down to the banks of the Danube where she had been shot, so that her body fell backwards into the black water, and drifted away among the blocks of ice.

As Kitty lay on her mattress in the small entrance lobby of Feri Skergula's apartment that night, finding it hard to sleep, worrying about her friend, the time was ticking towards midnight.

16

As SHE LAY HUDDLED under her eiderdown, trying to sleep (and failing) Kitty felt the minutes crawl past. Then came the sirens, raising their warning howl across the city. On the stairs could be heard the scurrying of the residents as they fled down to the air raid shelter. And then the distant droning of the high flying night bombers.

Before long the dull thud of falling bombs could be heard. The sounds grew closer. First would come the whistling noise of the falling bomb, and then the ground shuddering thud of its explosion.

'That one was close,' thought Kitty.

And then it came—a deafening crash that shook the building, and kept shaking it, like a toy in a giant's hand. The explosion made Kitty's ears ring. She pulled the eiderdown up over her head, but the crashing explosion did not stop—it rumbled on as a series of continuous crashes as bricks and masonry flew apart and crashed into the street below. The building trembled as the thumps and thuds continued. Kitty drew her knees up under her chin, and lay in a foetal position, every muscle tensed. Still the building shook, and the cracks and crashes continued. It seemed to last for minutes.

Then it stopped, and a silence settled over the city, like a heavy, black blanket—a silence that made you unwilling to be the first one to move, the first to speak.

Slowly, she pulled back the eiderdown. It was covered—she was covered—with dust and pieces of plaster from the walls and ceiling. Somewhere in the distance Kitty could hear someone screaming into the silence. The air raid was over. Kitty pushed back the eiderdown and tried to get to her feet. She was trembling, and her knees felt weak. She put a hand out to a wall to steady herself and felt a crack in the brick work that was several inches wide.

With shaking fingers she managed to find her small flashlight and flick it on. The air around her was filled with floating dust and flakes of plaster. Her ears were still ringing. As the air slowly cleared Kitty took a step forward and discovered that the floor of the small entrance lobby in which she had been trying to sleep was covered with rubble. The inner door to the living room of the apartment was standing partly open. The door frame was splintered—the explosion had blown it open.

Cautiously, she moved towards the door. As she did so a gust of icy wind blew it wide open. Kitty sheltered her flickering candle flame, took another step and looked through the open doorway. The outside wall of the apartment building was missing, and the floor of Feri Skergula's apartment now ended in a jagged, broken line ten feet away from where she was standing. As she had huddled on her mattress, under her eiderdown, she had been ten feet away from death.

With dazed unbelief Kitty looked at the night sky and the moonlight on the Danube. Quite suddenly she came to her senses.

'I must get out of here,' she muttered to herself. 'The building might collapse. It's not safe here. I must collect my things and move out. At once.'

Kitty realised she had been speaking aloud, even though there was no one to hear. She set the candle down in a protected corner and, with feverish hands, began packing up her few, and precious, belongings.

The eiderdown went back into its carry bag along with the small, black, iron cash box (the little it contained was now more precious than ever). Her clothes and personal items went into the one bag she had brought from her home. There was no chance of retrieving any food—that was in the kitchen and the floor leading to the kitchen had been blown away.

Kitty pulled on some warmer outer clothes, and tried to brush away some of the dust and plaster flakes that clung to everything.

She took one last look at the shattered apartment that had been her home for the last ten weeks, then pulled open the door leading to the stairs and left. For a moment the outer door jammed, as if its frame had been pushed out of shape, and for a brief moment of panic Kitty thought she might be trapped. But then it flew open with a rush, and she stepped out into the stairwell.

It was pitch black, so she went back and retrieved her flashlight to light her way through the rubble, broken bricks and pieces of masonry that littered the stairs.

When she emerged from the front door of number 3 Vigadó Square, Kitty saw a small, huddled group. One of the women was weeping. They were the other residents of the building, who had been in the air raid shelter as the bombs fell. They had emerged to discover half the building blown away and their homes gone.

One of the women saw Kitty and said, 'You too? Are you homeless too?' Kitty nodded, and the woman began to wail. The man beside her said, 'At least we're alive—alive and unhurt.'

That was when Kitty realised that she had not been injured. There were no pains and no bleeding. Her building had been bombed, and she was walking away from the damage unharmed.

'We've all had a narrow escape,' said the man, putting his arm around the woman beside him, presumably his wife. All Kitty could do was nod in agreement. She still felt dazed by the deafening blast—and amazed by her own survival.

She looked around. On the horizon was the flickering light of a fire set off by the bombs. For a moment she was uncertain what to do, and then she turned and walked down the street.

In one direction lay the Ritz Hotel—now a gutted ruin, destroyed by a bomb blast and fire a week ago. No point going in that direction. Kitty crossed Vigadó Square and kept on walking. She passed the ruins of the Hungaria and the Bristol hotels—both had been bombed in the ten weeks she had lived in Feri Skergula's apartment. Then came the Carlton Hotel. It was still standing, and in the pale blue moonlight Kitty could see people at the front door of the building.

She hastened her steps in that direction.

Pushing her way through a knot of uniformed *Nyilas* officers on the front steps, Kitty entered the lobby of the Carlton. The electricity was off, but the lobby was dimly lit by kerosene lamps.

Behind the reception desk was a clerk, an old man, too old to have been drafted into the army. He looked up from his book to see a dishevelled young woman, her face and clothes smeared with dust, flakes of plaster still clinging to her overcoat.

'I've just been bombed out,' she said quietly. 'I've just been bombed out at Vigadó Square. Can I have some shelter, please?'

For a long minute he didn't reply, then he said, 'There's a single room on the third floor—you can have that.'

He turned around and unhooked a key from a row of keys on the wall behind the reception desk. As he handed it over his face softened as he looked at the distraught, but pretty, young woman facing him.

'Come along, my dear,' he said, in a grandfatherly way, 'I'll show you where it is.'

The elderly clerk took a small flashlight from under the reception desk, and led the way to the stairs.

'No lift I'm afraid,' he muttered. 'Not since the last bombing raid destroyed the electricity power lines to the hotel.'

On the third floor he led her to the southern end of the corridor.

'Here it is,' he said. 'at the very end.'

He took the key out of Kitty's exhausted hand and unlocked the door for her.

'There's a candle on the bedside table. Do you have any matches, my dear?'

Too tired to speak, Kitty just nodded.

'The bathroom's at the end of the corridor, but there's a wash basin in the corner of the room. You should try to sleep, my dear.'

With that the old reception clerk left, closing the door as Kitty struck a match and lit the single candle in the room. It was a very plain room: a single bed, dressing table, a small wardrobe and a wash basin. There was no glass in the windows, of course—every window in central Budapest had been shattered by the bombing long before. But it was a room—it was somewhere to stay. She dropped her bags on the floor, pausing only to pull her warm eiderdown out of its carry bag.

I should wash my face and hands, she thought, but first I'll just lie down for a minute—I'm so tired, so very tired.

Kitty lay on the bed, and pulled the eiderdown up over her shoulders. The minute she lay down, she knew that she wouldn't be able to get up again for some hours. She reached out to where the single candlestick stood, close to the bed, blew out the candle, and rolled over. Then, from sheer exhaustion, she fell asleep.

*Churchill, Roosevelt and Stalin at the Yalta conference
in February 1945*

17

SHE SLEPT LATE THE next morning. When she finally awoke she was, for a moment, startled to find that she was not sleeping on the floor of Feri Skergula's apartment. Then it came back to her: the bombing raid, the explosion, the trudge through the moonlight to the Carlton Hotel. She stretched out her arms and legs, and then rolled over and slept again.

The next time she woke Kitty got out of bed and washed herself and brushed her hair. She pushed back the thick blackout curtains that covered the windows. The room she had been given was on a corner, with windows looking down on a small plaza. On the far side of the plaza was a beautiful old church. She recognised it as the oldest building in that part of the city.

It was an elegant building that spoke of Hungary's ancient civilisation. The church was first established during the reign of St István, the first king of Hungary. In the 14th century a large gothic church was built on the site, which was used as a Mosque when Hungary came under Turkish rule in the days of the Ottoman Empire. Damaged by the great fire of 1723, the church was partly rebuilt in the Baroque style by György Pauer in 1739.

Kitty loved beautiful things, and to be able to see something as beautiful as that building from her window was somehow reassuring—as if everything civilised in Europe was not going to end in rubble and flames.

Looking across the river she could see Gellert Hill, and rising from among the trees the monument to St Gellert, a bishop martyred in the 11th century. It was somehow comforting to be reminded that Budapest had existed long before this horror began—and would continue to exist long after it ended.

Before going downstairs Kitty took another look at herself in the mirror. Despite the brushing, washing and combing, she knew she still looked like an ally cat that had lost a fight.

Downstairs the lobby of the Carlton Hotel was in chaos. More homeless refugees had poured in after Kitty's arrival. There were people everywhere, all of them talking at once, some of them crying.

As she walked through the milling crowd Kitty realised that a number of these people were Jewish—like herself, Jews in hiding, pretending to be gentiles. But, she thought to herself, Jews can always recognise other Jews.

There were babies crying, small children running between the legs of the adults, and loud voices everywhere adding to the chaos. And there were uniforms, many uniforms. Some of them were *Nyilas*, others were German military uniforms.

Kitty wanted to know why there were so many Germans. Was there a German command post in the hotel? That was an alarming thought.

She turned around looking for someone to ask, and saw a young woman, about her own age—a stranger, but someone Kitty instinctively recognised as being Jewish.

'So many Germans,' said Kitty, careful not to raise her voice any more than she had to, to be heard over the din in the lobby. 'Why are there so many Germans here?'

'You must be new,' replied the young woman. 'There's a German Army First Aid Station downstairs, in the basement. Wounded German soldiers are coming and going the whole time. And, of course, there are some stationed here at the hotel permanently: German army surgeons and the like.'

Kitty looked around at the chaos, listened to the cascade of raised voices, and emotional voices, and shook her head in amazement.

'You'll get used to it,' said the young woman at her elbow

with a quiet laugh. 'By the way my name is Hedi—Hedi Zsolnai. And you are...?'

'Kitty—Kitty Kal...' Then Kitty remembered the false name she had written on the blank birth certificate she had purchased. 'Kovacs,' she corrected herself, 'Katalin Kovacs, but my friends call me "Kitty".'

'I thought so—you're also a...' her lips formed the word "Jew", and Kitty nodded in reply.

The two young women seemed to be the only calm people in that whole, crowded lobby. Everyone else seemed to be angry, or anxious, or trying to go somewhere or do something.

'Do the Germans pay much attention...?' asked Kitty, not finishing her question.

'To us, you mean?' responded Hedi, finishing the question for her. 'No, they're too busy losing the war. How do you come to be here?'

Kitty told her story: leaving their Jewish "yellow star" house, hiding in Feri Skergula's apartment, the bombing—everything. And then she asked Hedi for her story.

It turned out that Hedi was just two years younger than Kitty. Some years later—when the war was nothing but a horrible memory—Hedi was to become a famous singer in Budapest, known as "Hungary's Edith Piaf." But when Kitty first met her, she was just an innocent young girl. Hedi had come to the Carlton seeking shelter—exactly as Kitty had done.

Just then two young men in *Nyilas* uniforms pushed their way through the crowd and stood in front of the two pretty young women.

The shorter of the two took off his cap and said, 'Hello, Kitty—remember me?'

Kitty rapidly searched her memory, and then the name came back to her.

'It's Tivadar, isn't it?' she said.

'That's right. Tivadar de Govrik—we met at a party a few months ago. Or maybe it was more than a few months ago—I keep losing track of time in the war.'

Kitty smiled and shook his hand, but she was thinking, 'It was another world, another less frightening world in which we met.'

'Introduce me to your friend,' Tivadar was saying.

'This is Hedi.' Kitty made the introduction, and then asked, 'And who is this?'

The other young man was slightly taller, and a little more shy. Underneath a thick, peasant farmer's moustache Kitty instinctively recognised a Jewish face—yes, despite the Nyilas uniform Kitty was certain that this boy was Jewish.

'This is Tibor,' explained Tivadar. 'Tibor Kertesz.'

Tibor offered his hand and Kitty and Hedi both shook it.

'Can we get you two girls a hot drink?' Tivadar asked. 'There's no real tea and coffee of course, but on the other side of the lobby they have some planter tea or chicory—whichever you prefer.'

Kitty was starting to remember what it was like to be normal again, to have friends, to laugh, to enjoy the moment. The bitterness and anger that had been driving her for a while sank under layers of deliberate forgetfulness. She just wanted to be human again, to be young again.

Before long the four of them were drinking something hot and sweet and talking and flirting in the way that all young men and young women talk and flirt—war or no war, bombs or no bombs.

In the middle of their conversation, Tivadar suddenly shouted, 'Ah! They're back!'

Over the heads of the crowd in the lobby he had seen four young men in *Nyilas* uniforms come in through the front door. They were each carrying sacks. Tivadar shouldered his way through the crowd, spoke to the newcomers, got something from them, and pushed his way back again.

'Fresh bread rolls,' he announced, as he handed around what he had gathered to the small group. Kitty knew—they all knew—that the bread rolls came from a *Nyilas* raiding party that had just come back from looting shops. This was something they knew, but never spoke about.

That morning breakfast consisted of bread rolls and hot chicory in place of coffee. It was hardly a traditional meal for Christmas Day, but at least now Kitty was no longer alone. Now she had people with whom she could share the strange, unreal world Budapest had become as Russia's Red Army drew closer to the city, and the Germans prepared to evacuate.

18

OVER THE WEEKS THAT followed Kitty, Hedi, Tibor and Tivadar saw a lot of each other. Sometimes the two young men disappeared to take part in raiding parties. But they always shared the food they looted with the two girls. When Tibor and Tivadar were absent the girls would sit around and talk, either in Kitty's room or in Hedi's.

Once the boys came back with some cooked and salted beef, bread rolls, some cheese and a bottle of wine—and the four of them had a feast in Tibor's room. Another time they came back with a five kilogram box of sultanas—and this had to provide them with food for several days.

It quickly became apparent that Tivadar was particularly taken with Hedi, and that Tibor, in his shy way, was quite smitten by Kitty. The four of them spent a lot of time together— with structures and institutions falling apart, Tibor and Tivadar's official duties with the *Nyilas* seemed to take up very little of each day.

The air raids continued both night and day, but because the basement was occupied by the German Army First Aid station there was no air raid shelter, and so the inhabitants of the Carlton would gather in the lobby when the sirens sounded, and wait there until the raid was over.

During one such raid Kitty found herself in a corner of the lobby, sitting close to Tibor. Hedi and Tivadar had wandered off somewhere, and no one else was paying any attention to them.

Kitty seized the opportunity. 'Tibor,' she said, 'there's something I want to ask you.' He looked at her, smiled and nodded, but didn't say anything.

When she took her time asking her question he said, 'Well, what do you want to know?'

'You're Jewish,' said Kitty quietly. 'You're Jewish, aren't you?'

'You can tell?'

'A Jew can always tell another Jew. I don't know how, but we always can.'

There was another long silence before Tibor nodded and said, 'Yes. You're right.'

'So, why this?' asked Kitty, indicating his *Nyilas* uniform.

'My family were never religious Jews,' replied Tibor, looking uncomfortable. 'I never *felt* very Jewish. And it seemed...well... safe, I suppose. And all my friends were joining up.'

Kitty reached out and took his hand and gently squeezed it, to say: 'I understand.' But she didn't really understand. Tibor remained a mystery to Kitty—a puzzle, an enigma she never unravelled.

'I'm worried,' said Tibor, after a while.

'What about?'

'When the Russians come—the communists—they'll be hunting out the Hungarian fascists. Anyone in a *Nyilas* uniform will be a target. Somewhere I have to find some civilian clothes.'

'Don't you have any of your own civilian clothes?'

'No. My home was bombed. All I have to wear are my uniforms. They were at the barracks, so they survived when our house burned down.'

'I can get you some,' said Kitty excitedly.

'Where?'

'At my friend Feri's apartment. It was bombed, but his wardrobe was still standing when I left, and I know there's a suit and some shirts in there. And I think he's about your size too.'

'Then we must...' began Tibor.

Just then Hedi and Tivadar came back, and the conversation abruptly came to an end.

Two nights later the boys were out on patrol, and Kitty and Hedi were sitting in the lobby, drinking planter tea, and about to retire to bed, when Tibor came rushing in through the hotel's front door.

He looked around, spotted the two girls, and rushed over to them.

'Don't go to your own rooms tonight,' he said breathlessly. 'Go up to my room—here's the key.'

'But why...?' began Kitty.

'Don't ask. It will be safer, that's all. Both of you should sleep in my room tonight, to be safe.'

With those words he pushed a room key into Kitty's hand and was gone. Kitty and Hedi looked at each other, a little puzzled. But they knew Tibor would not have done this if it were not important, so that night they went to his room to settle down for the night. They talked until late, then blew out the candle and fell asleep.

It was sometime in the early hours of the morning when they were awoken by a loud pounding on the door. Struggling into consciousness from a deep sleep, Kitty got out of bed and felt her way through the darkness to the door. When she opened it she saw three young men standing there in *Nyilas* uniforms— Tibor was one of them. All three were armed and carried flashlights.

'Papers!' shouted the young officer leading the group. 'Identity papers! Immediately!'

Suddenly Kitty and Hedi were wide awake. This, they realised, was a Jew hunt. Kitty turned back into the room, and began to pretend to search for papers. Hedi did the same.

'Quick, quick!' shouted the officer. 'Papers!'

'But it's dark,' protested Kitty.

'We can't find our papers in the dark,' added Hedi.

'No excuses! Papers!'

'I don't know where I put my handbag,' Kitty complained, still pretending to search in the dark for her nonexistent papers.

Just then Tibor stepped forward and said, 'I know these two. They're all right.'

When the officer was slow to respond Tibor continued, 'Look, this is my room...and these girls are...well...friends of mine...if you know what I mean.'

At that the officer barked out a rough laugh and winked at Tibor, then he put his revolver back in his belt, nodded at the other two, and they moved on to the next room.

Kitty closed the door, breathing heavily. Hedi came over to her, and the two young women hugged in the darkened room. Both were trembling.

'We've escaped with our lives,' whispered Kitty.

'Just,' Hedi said. 'Only just.'

The next morning at breakfast time Kitty found Tibor in the lobby of the Carlton. She went over to him and placed her hand on his arm.

'I owe you my life,' she said softly.

He nodded, but said nothing.

'What happened last night?' asked Kitty. 'As a result of that search, what happened?'

'You don't want to know,' mumbled Tibor.

'Tell me.'

Tibor paused, and then said, 'Thirteen. Thirteen Jews were found without papers.'

'And...?'

'And they were taken out, lined up on the bank, and shot into the river.'

'Did you...?'

'No. I didn't have to do any of the shooting.'

As the days passed in the January of 1945 Tibor became more anxious about the advancing Russians, and more anxious for Kitty to take him to Feri Skergula's old apartment to find civilian clothing. The Russians were now on the outskirts of the city on the Pest side of the river, and the heavy artillery of the Red Army was shelling the city centre.

With the Russians so close the night bombing raids had stopped, but now the sirens sounded whenever the heavy artillery shelling began, and the people of Budapest hurried into their shelters as the shells whistled overhead and exploded into those buildings that were still standing.

The artillery attacks triggered off more fires, and by now there was no fire brigade to fight the fires, which were allowed to blaze out of control.

19

ON MONDAY, FEBRUARY 12, 1945, Kitty was standing at the wash basin in her room. She had washed her face and hands and brushed her hair when she heard the warning sirens begin their wail. Having just picked up her toothbrush she decided to stay at the basin and finish cleaning her teeth before she joined the others in the relative safety of the lobby. It was not a good decision.

Soon the shells could be heard whistling through the air, and the explosions began.

Kitty finished brushing her teeth, rinsed out her mouth and was just reaching for a towel when it happened. There was a massive explosion as a shell hit the plaza outside her window, and she felt as if a giant hand had picked her up and flung her across the room.

For a moment Kitty lost consciousness. As she lay on the floor where she had been thrown she gingerly tested her arms and legs. Everything seemed to move. Nothing seemed to be broken, and everything was still there. Carefully she raised herself to her knees. The room felt like a carousel spinning around, and her ears were ringing.

She knelt there for a time, leaning against the wall, then she grasped the edge of the dressing table and pulled herself upright. As she did so she felt something warm trickling down her face. She touched her forehead and then looked at her hand—it was covered in blood. On top of that, her forehead was starting to sting. Kitty wanted to look at herself in the mirror, to see what damage had been done, but the mirror was shattered.

On the floor she found a towel and held it up to the wound

in her head, and then, still half dazed and short of breath, she went out into the corridor. It was filled with people rushing about. None of them seemed to pay any attention to her. She headed for the stairs, and, clutching the hand rail tightly to steady herself, made her way down to the basement—to the German Army First Aid station.

The basement seemed to be even more chaotic than the hotel above. There were people being treated everywhere—as many civilians as soldiers. A room at one end of the basement appeared to have been turned into an operating theatre. A surgeon hurried out, blood all over his surgical gown, pulled off his stained gloves, put on a fresh pair, and rushed back in.

An orderly saw that Kitty was dazed and uncertain on her feet. Because of her time in Vienna, Kitty was able to talk to him in fluent German.

'I need help,' she said faintly. And then she pointed out the obvious by adding, 'My head is bleeding.'

The orderly took her arm and led her to a chair. He gently but forcefully pulled away the hand that was holding the blood soaked towel to her forehead and examined the wound.

'It's not too bad,' he announced, 'but it will need stitches. Is anything broken, do you have any other injuries?'

'No...at least, I don't think so.'

The young orderly felt the major bones in Kitty's arms and legs, and then said, 'Move your fingers for me, and wiggle your toes.'

Kitty did as she was told.

'Everything else is fine—as far as I can tell without an X-ray, and we have no X-ray,' said the orderly.

He left and came back a moment later with a basin and some cotton wool, and proceeded to clean the wound with antiseptic that stung and made Kitty wince.

'There,' he said a moment later, 'that's done. Hold this

against the wound to stop the bleeding until a doctor is free to take a look at you.'

He pressed a pad of gauze into Kitty's hand. Kitty held this against her forehead, while people rushed around her shouting orders as more and more wounded arrived. She was sitting quite close to the operating theatre door. As she glanced around she noticed a basket not far away. At first she couldn't quite understand what she was seeing, and then it came into focus. It was a basket filled with bullet and bomb shattered limbs that had been amputated. The wicker basket was a jumble of severed hands, arms, feet and legs.

Half an hour later a doctor came over, looked at her wound, and ordered that a local anaesthetic be applied. The orderly did this, and then the doctor returned with surgical needle and thread.

He muttered to himself in German while he did his work, and then said, 'Two stitches—that's all it needs. Orderly, dress this wound!'

A different orderly came up, a big, clumsy man who proceeded to wind layers of bandages around Kitty's head. He finished off one roll of surgical bandages, pinned it in place, and then fetched another, and wound even more layers of bandage around Kitty's head.

Surely the wound is not as bad as all that? she thought to herself.

Eventually he was finished, and told her brusquely, in German, that she could go. As she walked towards the stairs Kitty tried to discover what he had done and what she now looked like. There were no mirrors, so she gently passed a hand over the wrappings. The bandages seemed to run everywhere. They wound around her head, back and front, and under her chin and over the top of her head.

She shook her head in disbelief at the alien creature she

knew she must look like. 'I must look like an Egyptian mummy,' she muttered to herself. 'Something that's just been dragged out of a tomb.'

Kitty made her way up the basement stairs to the lobby. There she found Hedi and Tibor anxiously looking for her. Hedi went pale at the sight of her heavily bandaged head, and Tibor slipped an arm around her and kept asking how she felt.

'It looks worse than it is,' said Kitty firmly. 'A fool of a German orderly has put far more bandages on me than I need.'

At length she succeeded in persuading both of them that her wound was only minor.

'Well,' said Hedi, 'we can't stay here any longer. Certainly you can't, Kitty—your room is a mess.'

'Let's go back to your friend's apartment building,' urged Tibor. 'I'll get some civilian clothes out of his bombed apartment, and then we can take up temporary residence in the bomb shelter in the basement at Vigadó Square.'

Hedi agreed that this was a good idea.

'But what about Tivadar?' Kitty asked.

'He's taken off,' explained Tibor. 'He's gone back to his home in the suburbs to change into civilian clothes and wait for the Russians to come. We won't see him for a while.'

Tibor and Hedi both went upstairs—Hedi to collect her things from her room, and Tibor to collect both his own things and Kitty's things. They made Kitty rest on a chair in the lobby like an invalid.

When they returned the three of them set off for Vigadó Square to await the arrival of the Russians.

20

STANDING AT THE FRONT door of the Carlton Hotel Kitty could see that it was snowing—had been snowing for some time, with snow thickly covering the streets and deep drifts building up against the walls.

She stopped to open up her suitcase, take out a woollen scarf and tie it over her head.

'It will stop the bandages from getting soaking wet from the snow,' she explained to the others, and then the three of them stepped out into the snow and turned towards Vigadó Square. It was slow going through the drifts and the swirling, driving snow. Whipped by winter winds, the snow stung their faces. The wind was blowing directly off the black, freezing water of the Danube, filled, at this time of year, with drifting blocks of ice.

They hadn't gone far down the street when Hedi grabbed Kitty's arm and said, 'Look! The bridges.'

From where they were they could see up and down the sweep of the river that divided Budapest, and they could see that all the bridges—ancient and beautiful bridges—that had linked the two halves of the city were gone.

'The Germans blew up the last of the bridges yesterday,' Tibor explained, 'to slow down the Russian advance.' Allied bombing had already destroyed the others.

As they hurried on through the snow they could hear the sound of sporadic gunfire coming from the opposite side of the river—the Buda side.

'The Russians already control Buda,' said Tibor. 'They're probably shooting *Nyilas*.' As he spoke he glanced down at his own *Nyilas* uniform, and walked more briskly and purposefully through the snow.

Kitty blinked in the wind and falling snow and stared across the river. She could just make out a flag flapping vigorously in the strong wind on a flagpole on Castle Hill. In place of the Swastika the flag showed the communist emblem of the hammer and sickle.

Further up the river there was activity on the opposite bank that attracted Tibor's attention. He shielded his eyes from the glare of the snow and stared for a minute, before saying, 'Those are Russian army engineers. They're beginning to lay a pontoon bridge. The Red Army will be here tomorrow—the Germans are sure to leave today. You were lucky to find the German army first aid station still functioning, Kitty.'

In fact, the Germans failed to retreat quickly enough before the advancing Russians, and 110,000 of them were taken prisoner over the next 24 hours.

Hedi, who had few warm clothes, was starting to shiver, and so the three hurried the rest of the way, and stepped into the front door of number 3 Vigadó Square with relief.

Kitty pushed the scarf back off her head saying, 'It's so good to be out of that wind.'

She stood for a moment, listening to the wind howling around the building—the only sound that could be heard.

'It's very quiet,' said Hedi, through chattering teeth.

'I wonder where everyone's gone?' Kitty puzzled.

'They've left the city,' muttered Tibor, 'if they've got any sense.'

'Where to first?' asked Kitty. 'The air raid shelter?'

'I've got to get out of these clothes,' snapped Tibor, nervously fingering his *Nyilas* uniform.

'Come on then,' Kitty responded, leading the way up the stairs to the first floor. Their footsteps awoke echoes in the empty building.

The door to Feri Skergula's apartment was still standing ajar, just as Kitty had left it on the night she had fled. She pushed it wide open and led Hedi and Tibor into the small entrance lobby of the apartment in which she had lived for more than two months.

'Where are those civilian clothes you were telling me about?' urged Tibor.

'Through here,' replied Kitty, leading the way into what was left of the living room in the apartment.

'I'm not going in there,' said Hedi nervously, pulling back. 'There's no outside wall. That floor might collapse at any time.'

'Well, I am,' Tibor said firmly. 'Unless I get out of this uniform the Russians will shoot me the minute they see me. Where are the clothes kept?'

Kitty led the way to the wardrobe that stood on what remained of the apartment floor. Wind had blown snow into the living room, and small drifts of snow had piled up in the corners. Opening the wardrobe doors Kitty pointed to a suitcase on a top shelf. Tibor reached up and pulled the case down with a grunt of effort. It was not locked, and a moment later he was rummaging through its contents, looking for suitable civilian clothing.

Meanwhile, Kitty was hunting through the back of the wardrobe.

'I left some clothes here,' she explained. 'I couldn't carry everything with me when I fled. I'm sure I can find something warm here for Hedi.'

Tibor was not listening. From Feri's suitcase he had extracted a sports coat, a pair of trousers, and two shirts.

'These will do,' he muttered with satisfaction. 'And they look to be about the right size too. Well, close enough.'

Kitty had found a warm winter coat, and she took this back to where Hedi was waiting for them, in the entrance lobby.

'Here, try this on. I think it will fit you,' said Kitty.

'Oh, it's so nice and thick,' whispered Hedi through chattering teeth and she pulled on the coat. 'Oh, it's so warm, Kitty. Are you sure you can spare it?'

'Yes, yes, I have enough clothes to stay warm. Are you coming, Tibor?'

'I'm just getting changed,' Tibor shouted from the next room. 'I'll leave my *Nyilas* uniform up here. If the Russians find it anywhere near me, they might work out that I have been a *Nyilas* officer.'

The two girls waited while Tibor went into the bathroom and changed his clothes. They stamped their feet and slapped their sides with their arms to try to keep warm.

'A nice warm coat,' said Hedi, 'and the Russians coming to protect us from the Nazis—we're going to be all right Kitty, everything's going to be all right. I must make myself look nice for the Russians.'

With these words Hedi opened up her handbag and took out a small mirror and a comb, and began to do her hair and tidy up her appearance as best she could.

'I've just remembered,' Hedi said, as she continued to fix her appearance, 'someone told me the Russian word for "Jewish"— I'll teach you and Tibor. We must shout it out when the Russians come. Let them know that we are Jewish—that we have been victims of the Nazis. They will be sympathetic, I know they will.'

Just then Tibor emerged from the bomb shattered remains of the living room. He had pulled his heavy overcoat over Feri Skergula's clothes.

'How do I look?' he asked. 'Like a real civilian, eh?'

'You look simply wonderful,' replied Kitty with a laugh. 'Come on now—down to the air raid shelter, and out of this freezing cold apartment.'

The young man and the two young women made their way

back down the staircase—still littered with broken bricks and pieces of masonry from the last bombing raid. When they reached the ground floor they kept on going down another level, for the air raid shelter was simply the cellar of the apartment building.

21

KITTY LED THE WAY, and when she reached the cellar and opened the door she reached inside for the light switch and then stopped—the light was already on.

'The electricity is back on...for this building, at any rate,' Hedi remarked, with a note of surprise in her voice.

'Someone one must be here,' said Kitty, 'or else the light was left on when everyone left after that night when the bomb damaged the building.'

Descending the last flight of stairs Kitty looked around. It was an ordinary cellar with brick walls and floor. There was one electric light bulb dangling from a cord in the middle of the ceiling throwing a dim yellow light and patches of dark shadow around the cellar. Part of the area of was divided into separate storage spaces—one for each apartment above—by simple wire cages. Most of these had once held coal or wood for heating; most were now empty.

In a far corner of the cellar there was movement in the shadow, and then two people emerged: a young man and a young woman.

The two groups stared at each other suspiciously for a moment, deep suspicion being a legacy of years of war.

After a time the young man said, nervously, 'Hello. Are you going to stay here? In the cellar?'

'Where's everyone else?' asked Kitty.

'The building was empty when we came,' replied the young man. Then he turned to the young woman at his side and said, 'This is my wife.'

But, Kitty noticed, he didn't introduce himself, or tell them his wife's name.

'We're staying here until the Germans have all gone, and the

Russians have arrived,' announced Tibor firmly.

With that the young couple retreated to their corner and held a whispered conversation.

Kitty and Hedi searched around the rest of the small cellar.

'Look here!' called out Hedi. 'Look what I've found.'

Kitty and Tibor hurried to her side and saw that she was pointing at one of the storage cages that was piled high with rolled up Persian rugs.

'We can spread these on the floor,' said Kitty, sharing Hedi's excitement, 'and they'll keep us warm.'

Soon several layers of thick, beautifully made Persian rugs had been spread across the middle of the cellar floor. Tibor carried one of the rugs over to the young couple in the corner. They accepted it gratefully with a word of thanks.

'Who are they?' whispered Hedi.

Tibor shrugged his shoulders and said, 'Just refugees.'

'Like us,' added Kitty.

'Yes,' agreed Tibor, 'refugees like us, and afraid of everyone.'

Once they were settled down on the rugs, wrapped up in warm clothes, Kitty, Hedi and Tibor relaxed. They had got out of the hotel that held a German army unit; Tibor was in civilian clothes; they were dry and if not exactly warm at least they were less cold than they had been. All they had to do now was wait for the liberation of Budapest by the Red Army.

Once again Hedi took a small mirror out of her handbag and began applying a little of the makeup she had left.

'I want to make myself look nice,' she said. 'I'm tired of looking untidy and grubby and unattractive.'

Kitty ran her fingers lightly over the thick layers of bandages that were wrapped about her head in every direction.

'I don't think I can manage that,' she said with a smile. 'At least, not until these bandages come off. I'm going to have to put up with looking horrible for a while longer.'

'You look like an Egyptian mummy,' Tibor said with a laugh. 'You would delight any passing archaeologist.' And then he added, 'but when the bandages come off you'll look as pretty as ever.'

Tibor went outside with an empty can and filled it with snow. This he brought back to the cellar and sat it between the three of them to melt, so they would, at least, have water to drink.

'All that food you and Tivadar looted—do you have any of it left?' Kitty asked.

Tibor rummaged around in a bag he was carrying before replying, 'A few bread rolls, stale now I think, and the remains of that box of sultanas.'

'I don't ever want to eat sultanas again,' Kitty said, pulling a face.

But they did eat sultanas again, and washed them down with water from the melted snow. They stayed in the cellar for the rest of that day and the night that followed—getting very little sleep on the cold hard floor. The other couple seemed to have a little food of their own, and they kept quietly to themselves throughout the night.

In that cellar the only sense of passing time came from Tibor's wristwatch. When the watch told them that the night had passed and morning had come Kitty suggested, 'Why don't you go outside, and see what's happening?'

'Not in my civilian clothes,' responded Tibor. 'Not until I know the Russians have come. If the Russians aren't here yet, and the *Nyilas* catch me in mufti...well...'

He didn't need to finish the sentence, because all three of them knew that the *Nyilas* guards had now collapsed into being little more than roaming gangs of murderers.

'I'll go and look,' volunteered Hedi.

Pulling the warm coat that Kitty had given her tightly around her shoulders, Hedi mounted the cellar steps and disappeared from view.

Within two minutes she was back, shouting excitedly, 'They're here! The Russians are here!' then she turned around and rushed back up the steps.

Kitty and Tibor followed her, and they could hear the other young couple from the cellar on their heels.

They burst out into the sunlight to be dazzled by the thick layers of white snow that covered the ground and piled up against every building. As their eyes adjusted they blinked in disbelief at the change from yesterday: the streets were now filled with people, and with Russian soldiers.

Troop transport trucks rumbled past, painted dark battleship grey and marked with the hammer and sickle insignia in bright red and yellow paint. The small group in front of number 3 Vigadó Square cheered and waved. The truck drivers waved back, and the soldiers who could be seen in the back of the trucks grinned widely and shouted something unintelligible in Russian.

'The Russian word for "Jewish",' Hedi yelled excitedly to Kitty and Tibor. 'Remember, I taught it to you? Shout it out, now.'

All three of them shouted, and laughed, and cheered and waved.

'I am just so happy,' said Kitty, tears of joy trickling down her cheeks and soaking into her bandages. 'It's over...it's over... really over.'

Just then, at some distance away they heard some sporadic shooting.

Kitty said nothing out loud, but silently, to herself, she said, 'Almost over.'

There were Russians everywhere. A Russian foot patrol marching on the far side of Vigadó Square called out and waved in response to the greetings of the liberated people of Budapest. There were troops everywhere. Some of them were Cossacks on horseback, and some were riding on tanks. And there were trucks beyond counting—one after another seemed to pass by in an endless stream.

Looking around the skyline of the city Kitty could see that all the Nazi Swastika flags had disappeared and been replaced by the Red Army flag—a red flag bearing the hammer and sickle insignia in yellow.

For a long time the small group from the cellar of number 3 Vigadó Square stood in the streets waving and cheering and welcoming their liberators. After an hour or so their throats were getting hoarse from laughing and cheering, the snow had made them damp, and the cold was starting to seep through their clothing.

'We might as well go back to the cellar,' said Tibor, 'and give these fellows a chance to settle in and take control. Wait until the last of the shooting stops. Then we'll go out and find some-where more comfortable, and, if we're lucky, some decent food to eat.'

This was sensible, and so Kitty, Tibor and Hedi returned to their dry cellar to wait a little longer. The young couple with whom they'd shared their cellar followed their example.

For the next few hours they sat in the cellar talking and making plans.

'Where can we go from here?' Hedi asked.

'Well,' suggested Kitty, 'once the streets are safe again we can go back to my apartment in Academia Street.'

Tibor strongly approved of this plan, and started discussing when it would be safe to make a move.

While they were talking they heard sounds upstairs—heavy army boots in the entrance hall, and then thumping down the cellar stairs. They felt no alarm—these were the Russians, their liberators, and they prepared to greet them with smiles and handshakes.

Then the soldiers arrived in the cellar. Russian soldiers. Kitty was never sure how many there were—ten, perhaps twelve. They arrived grim faced. They did not look exactly like liberators. Two of them had their revolvers drawn. Several of them were handing around a bottle of vodka.

They looked around the cellar and quickly summed up the situation. A soldier, a huge beefy man, grabbed Hedi and dragged her over to the corner where the young couple had been sleeping. Here he threw her roughly on to the Persian rug that lay there.

Tibor began to loudly protest, but one of the soldiers raised his revolver and cocked the hammer. Tibor fell silent. Kitty found herself looking down the barrel of a revolver for the first time in her life.

The young man, the husband, suddenly landed beside them. He had been roughly flung there by one of the soldiers. He began to protest loudly in Hungarian. The soldiers barked at him in Russian and laughed—a cruel and mirthless laugh. Tibor, Kitty and the young husband were guarded by two soldiers—both armed with revolvers.

Kitty couldn't see what was happening to Hedi, or to the young wife, but she heard them scream—and then heard the screams stop, as if muffled by a large hand. Latter she heard the sobbing, pleading, and crying.

Both women were raped, repeatedly, by that group of Russian soldiers.

The men with the revolvers handed their guns over to their comrades, so they could take their turn, while someone else stood guard over the three prisoners at the far end of the cellar.

Kitty turned to Tibor, her face as pale as her bandages.

'Why...?' she began.

'Sshh!' hissed Tibor. 'It's those bandages—those and the heavy winter clothes you're wearing. They think you're a man.'

Kitty went to speak, but Tibor laid a finger on her lips.

'Don't speak,' whispered Tibor urgently. 'Don't let them hear your voice. As long as they don't know you're a girl, you're safe. There's nothing we can do for poor Hedi...'

His voice trailed away at the sickening thought of what Hedi was going through.

Tears filled Kitty's eyes. She just wanted it to stop.

'Poor, poor Hedi,' she thought. 'Please, please, let it stop.'

It was a nightmare, a black, horrible nightmare. Kitty didn't know, couldn't know, exactly what Hedi was going through, but she could guess, she did guess, and every sob, every cry seemed to tear at her heart. It was another burden to add to the load of bitter anger her heart already bore. Was there no end to the evil that human nature was capable of.

Eventually, it was over.

The soldiers trooped out of the cellar, the armed guards being the last to leave, barking incomprehensible orders in Russian over their shoulders as they departed. Kitty rushed over to Hedi's side.

Hedi was hysterical. She was crying, weeping, sobbing loudly. Kitty gathered up Hedi's clothes, some of which had been torn. She was shocked to see how badly beaten and bruised Hedi's body was. At first Kitty just took Hedi in her arms and held her as she wept hysterically. Hedi clung to her, like a baby clinging to a mother.

'I just want to die,' she sobbed, 'I just want to die.'

Kitty hugged her and tried to comfort her.

22

TIBOR GATHERED UP their meagre belongings that were scatted around the cellar.

'We can't stay here,' he said. 'It's not safe. We'll have to move out.'

'Soon, soon,' Kitty replied. 'In a little while. When Hedi is feeling a little better.'

The husband was leading his wife up the stairs while this conversation was going on.

'I'm taking my wife to a doctor,' he said. 'She needs a doctor.'

'That's what you need, Hedi,' said Kitty quietly, as soothingly as she could. 'I have to get you to a doctor.'

'Where will we find a doctor?' asked Tibor anxiously.

Kitty thought for a moment and then said, 'In our apartment building—in Academia Street. There's a doctor in our building. At least there was. We can start there.'

Tibor agreed, and finished packing up their meagre belongings.

As Hedi began to calm down a little Kitty helped her to get dressed in warm clothing, and then helped her to her feet.

Hedi was still sobbing in a way that broke Kitty's heart. She clung to Kitty for support like a frightened child. Slowly and gently Kitty led her to the cellar steps, and then out into the bleak winter sunshine.

It was about the middle of the day. There were still some soldiers about in Vigadó Square, but not nearly as many as there had been earlier in the morning. At the sight of their uniforms Hedi flinched, and began to cry again. Kitty took one arm, and Tibor the other, and, together, they encouraged her to start walking—however painful it might be.

Soon they were pushing through the thick falls of snow down Dorotya Street towards Academia Street.

Progress was slow, Hedi was exhausted, and the snow was heavy. Before they were halfway to their destination, snow began falling again. In the streets around them they were aware of the movement of Russian troops. On one street corner a Red Army soldier spoke to them in Russian. They could do nothing except to shrug their shoulders and indicate that they couldn't understand. He was a young man, very young for a soldier, and he looked concerned, but when he realised that communication was impossible, he too shrugged his shoulders and went on his way.

Hedi's body still trembled with her sobbing, but she was not crying aloud any longer, and the hysteria appeared to be slowly fading.

At one point Hedi stumbled and Kitty had to catch her so that she wouldn't fall. As she stood there catching her breath, Hedi said, 'I thought they'd kill me.'

Kitty took her friend's hand and squeezed it. She could find no words to say.

Tibor put his arm around Hedi's waist, and took as much of her weight as he could. In this manner they pushed on through the freezing cold that was beginning to seep through their thick winter clothes.

They crossed over Zrínyi Street and came to Arany János Street.

'We're almost there,' said Kitty encouragingly. 'Almost there, Hedi. In a little while we'll find you a doctor and get you some help.'

For another block they pushed their way through increasingly heavy snow drifts, and then they reached the corner of Academia and Széchenyi Streets.

'There it is,' said Kitty. 'That's my apartment building, on the corner opposite. Just a few more steps, Hedi—we're almost there.'

As they stepped out on to the road, Kitty looked up to her right and saw a lone figure approaching them down the deserted, snow-covered pavement. It was a small, grey figure with a bent back.

Although nothing but a silhouette against the blindingly white snow, somehow that figure looked familiar to Kitty. Surely it wasn't...? It couldn't be! But, yes, it was!

'Tibor,' said Kitty urgently, 'look after Hedi.'

Letting Tibor take all of Hedi's weight, Kitty turned and ran towards the small figure that was approaching.

The cold air was painful in her lungs as she ran, but as she drew closer Kitty saw that she hadn't been mistaken.

'Mama!' she cried out. 'Mama!'

The small grey figure, looking so intently down at the snow and at where she was placing her feet, looked up—at first puzzled, and then pleased. And then mother and daughter were in each other's arms.

'Oh, mama, mama,' sobbed Kitty as she held her mother for the first time in months.

The two women wept and laughed and hugged each other.

'Are you all right, Kitty?' asked Ada. 'Those bandages...have you been hurt?'

'I'm fine, mama. It's just a little scratch. A German army surgeon put two stitches in for me.'

'A German? A German? Where have you been, Kitty? What has been happening to you?'

'It's a long story, mama, I'll tell you soon. But are you all right? Where have you been?'

'In the ghetto—in the Jewish ghetto until the Russians came this morning and opened the gates and pulled down the barbed wire.'

'Have you been hurt? Are you all right?'

'Only my feet. They are hurting me, Kitty. I think it's frost bite.'

'Then we must get you inside as quickly as possible, and out of this snow.'

Kitty took them in through the front door of her old apartment building.

Once inside, and out of the snow and the damp, she made the introductions: explaining to Ada just who Hedi and Tibor were and how she had met them, and introducing her two friends to her mother. Then Kitty led the group upstairs—Kitty supporting Ada, and Tibor supporting Hedi.

'There's a doctor on the same floor as our apartment, Hedi,' said Kitty as they mounted the stairs. 'We'll get some help for you in a just a minute or two.'

Kitty noticed that while she, Tibor and Hedi were carrying bundles and suitcases (like refugees or gypsies, she thought) Ada was empty-handed.

'You have brought no possessions with you, mama?' she asked.

'I just wanted to come home,' said Ada quietly. 'As soon as they let us out, I just wanted to come home.'

As she said this she took a key out of her pocket and unlocked the front door of the apartment.

They walked inside.

To Kitty her old home looked so empty, dark and deserted. The glass was missing from all the windows—presumably destroyed during the recent shelling—and the wooden shutters were closed. Kitty walked over and pushed open the shutters. But as she did so, the window collapsed, raining debris around her.

'It's a shambles,' said Ada sadly. 'Most of the furniture is missing.'

'It would have been burned as fuel, to heat the place,' suggested Tibor, nodding at the large, ceramic-tile-covered wood-burning heater that stood in the corner.

'Most probably,' agreed Ada, nodding, then she looked more closely at her daughter and said, 'You're dressed in rags, Kitty—nothing but rags.'

'So are you, mama,' replied Kitty with a laugh. 'So are we all. We're filthy and we're dressed in rags—but the war is over, and things will get better.'

Kitty walked from room to room, looking at the shambles that their apartment was in. She found the beds were the only large pieces of furniture that hadn't been burned, so she took Hedi gently by the arm and led her to a bed.

'Here, Hedi love,' said Kitty, 'lie down here and rest while I find out if the doctor is still next door. And mama, you must sit down and try to get your feet warm.'

Kitty went back out into the corridor and knocked loudly on the front door of the next apartment. There was no answer so she tried the door handle—it was unlocked. Stepping inside she discovered the apartment empty and deserted.

'The doctor is no longer there,' she reported when she returned to the others.

'He was Jewish,' said Ada, 'he must have been deported.'

'But we must find a doctor for poor Hedi,' said Kitty, anxiously.

'There's an old gentile doctor who lived not far away,' Ada suggested. 'He is almost certain to still be there.'

Ada gave Kitty an address in Arany János Street.

'Come along, Tibor,' said Kitty, 'we must take Hedi there at once.'

The two of them helped Hedi off the bed, rugged her up against the cold and took her the block and a half to the doctor's surgery. He was an old man, but he was there, and his surgery was still intact.

He treated Hedi, and then Kitty and Tibor took her back to

the apartment.

Hedi stayed with them for one more day, and then announced that she was feeling much better, and wanted to go back to her parent's house. Tibor offered to walk her there.

Then Tibor returned. In fact, Tibor showed no interest in leaving. And Tibor was about to become a major problem for Kitty and Ada.

Hedi Zsolnai

23

OVER THE NEXT FEW days Kitty, Ada and Tibor managed to salvage some furniture from abandoned or bombed out apartments. Some of it was damaged and all of it was battered, but it was adequate.

They also purchased food—a bag of rice and some tins of food—at exorbitant prices on the black market. At this time, with the currency so unstable, purchases usually had to be paid for in gold—either one of the dwindling supply of gold napoleons in their cash box, or a link broken off from a gold necklace.

Tibor showed no sign of leaving, and no interest in returning to his own people or finding out what had happened to them in the last, dreadful days of the war. Indeed, with every hour that passed he looked more settled.

When they returned from the black market shopping expedition he turned to Ada and said, 'Perhaps I'd better start calling you "Mama"—since you're going to be my mother-in-law.'

A startled Ada dragged Kitty into one of the bedrooms for a whispered conversation.

'You didn't tell me you were engaged,' hissed Ada.

'I'm not engaged.'

'But, Tibor said...'

'I heard what Tibor said. But he hasn't said anything to me. He most certainly hasn't proposed.'

'He seems to be taking it for granted.'

'Perhaps,' said Kitty anxiously, 'it's just his way. He's not very sophisticated.' Then she added petulantly, 'He looks like a peasant and he behaves like a peasant.'

'Kitty! He saved your life.'

'Yes, yes, Mama—I know he saved my life and I'm very, very grateful. But he can't expect me to marry him, just because I'm grateful.'

But he did. That fact became clearer as the days passed. Kitty and Ada became desperate to get Tibor out of the apartment. If only he would leave, they thought, he might forget about Kitty. But so much of the city had been destroyed by the bombing, accommodation was scarce. Tibor could justify sleeping in their spare bedroom because there was nowhere else to go. Well, nowhere obvious at least, and Tibor wasn't looking for anywhere.

The Russian conquest of Hungary was part of the final assault on Germany. Soviet soldiers continued the march westward, driving the German army before them, across Hungary, through Austria, and into Germany itself. The Red Army had reached the Oder River, 65 kilometres east of Berlin, by the end of January, 1945. At the same time Allied forces in the west were moving forward. They occupied positions along the Rhine by early March.

As they advanced, the Allies discovered the horrifying evidence of Nazi brutality. They saw with their own eyes the grim evidence of the death camps, and Hitler's ghastly plans for the Jews—his "final solution to the Jewish question".

As the Russian Army continued to pour into Budapest, in February, 1945, they imposed martial law and brought the roving gangs of *Nyilas* thugs under control. Then officials and administrators who had survived the last days of the war came out of hiding, and the slow process of restoring the administration and institutions of the city began.

The Red Army needed to accommodate the thousands of troops it was bringing into the city. An entire apartment block, one of the less bomb damaged buildings, a few streets away from Academia Street, was requisitioned for a company of Russian marines—and all the Hungarian inhabitants of the building were turned out to make way for the soldiers.

Russian officers went from door to door looking for apartments, or spare rooms, they could requisition. Inevitably, they came to Kitty and Ada's apartment.

It was Kitty who responded to the insistent knocking. She recognised the uniform.

'We are commandeering needed accommodation,' the Russian officer explained in heavily accented Hungarian.

Before he could say something about taking over the whole apartment and ordering them onto the street, Kitty volunteered, 'Our maid's room is empty. We would be more than happy to billet one of your men.' This was greeted by silence, so Kitty hurriedly continued, 'It's a very good room. Self-contained. It has its own entrance.'

There was a long pause, and then the officer said, 'That will do.' He barked something in Russian to the young private beside him, who made a note in a notebook. 'Your billet will arrive within 24 hours,' he announced, then saluted, turned and departed.

The following afternoon Anatole arrived. Kitty and Ada never learned to pronounce his surname, so he was always just Anatole to them. He was a sergeant in the Russian marines, a beefy man in his mid thirties. He was a gentle, quietly spoken man who managed to communicate using his few words of Hungarian and a lot of sign language.

His first act on being shown his room endeared him at once to Kitty and Ada—he took a battered black and white photograph of his wife and children out of his pocket, and placed it on the bedside table.

Anatole turned out to be a treasure: when he realised that food was so scarce, every day he brought a little food from the Russian army canteen back to the apartment. Most days it was a type of Russian pie called *pirozhki*. These triangles of pastry were filled with vegetables, and, some days, with meat as well. It came wrapped in a piece of newspaper, as a rule, but it was food, and it was fresh, and Kitty and Ada were very grateful. Anatole also brought Russian tea, and, on some days, oranges or other fruit.

However, the problem of Tibor remained to be solved.

Kitty and her mother slept in one of the main bedrooms of the apartment, Tibor had camped in the other, and Anatole was using what had been the maid's room. Kitty wanted to be free of Tibor's attentions, and his insistence that she would marry him: Ada wanted him out of her apartment.

Tibor was often out during the day, meeting people, making contacts, and organising his own future. For all his lack of sophistication and peasant ways he was a clever and cunning man. His father had been a communist for many years (long before the war) and as Tibor quickly saw which way the tide was running he announced that he was now a communist too. In fact, he claimed to have been a communist sympathiser all along. Kitty realised that it would be wise not to ask him why, if he'd been a communist sympathiser, he'd joined the fascists, so she kept quiet on that subject.

'You must become a communist,' Tibor announced to Kitty.

'But I have no interest in politics,' she protested.

'That doesn't matter,' interrupted Tibor, raising his hand to silence her. 'If I am to advance in the Party I must have a good communist wife. You must join the party.'

'But, I have no interest...'

Ignoring her protests he continued, 'I have arranged an interview for you with the membership secretary at Party headquarters for tomorrow afternoon. I shall take you there myself. And my father will be there, he will vouch for you—that will make it certain that you are accepted as a member.'

When she was alone with her mother Kitty asked, 'What shall I do?'

Ada shrugged, 'We are just two women—what can we do? When your father comes home from the German prison camp, he will know what to do.'

But Papa would not be back the next day when Kitty was to be enrolled in the Communist Party.

After lunch on the following day Tibor marched Kitty through the streets, that were slowly being cleared of rubble and burned-out ruins, to the office building that was the head-quarters of the Hungarian Communist Party on Andrassy Street. Here they were met by Tibor's father, who was even more of a peasant than his son, Kitty decided—he was a gruff and brusque man. She was taken upstairs by the two men to the office occupied by the membership secretary—a bald man with wire-framed spectacles.

As she sat down in an office chair the secretary pulled out an impressive looking membership form, and began to ask a long series of questions. As soon as she grasped that these questions were directed towards her suitability to become a member of the Party, Kitty understood what she had to do. In answer after answer she stressed that she came from a bourgeois family, that all her father's friends were wealthy capitalists, that her parents had been prominent in pre-war social circles, that her father had been a highly paid professional, that she had been to a private school. Each of these answers seemed to irritate the little membership secretary more than the last. At length his face went quite red, he angrily crumpled up the half-completed membership form, and said, 'Rejected! This young woman is most unsuitable for the Hungarian Communist Party.'

Tibor's father swore at his son, calling him several kinds of a fool. Tibor marched Kitty back downstairs, out into the street, and back to the apartment in sullen silence. Kitty had managed to hold off the communist party, but Tibor seemed to remain as determined as ever to marry her.

However, for the moment, the problem of getting rid of Tibor was put to one side as Kitty and Ada hoped for Aladar's return from the German prison camps. The camps had been liberated by the Americans, and slowly the Jewish prisoners were arriving back in Budapest, a few more each day.

'There are no clothes,' said Ada one day. 'All of Aladar's clothes are gone. We must buy him some before he comes home. He will have nothing but wretched prison clothing when he comes back.'

The next day the two women took one of their precious gold napoleons out of the cash box, and by going around to a number of black market dealers, managed to buy a suit, several shirts, under clothes, socks, and a pair of shoes.

'It won't be long now,' said Ada, they placed their new purchases in a wardrobe in the apartment. 'Aladar will be home soon.'

Each new arrival from the camps they pestered for information. Which camp had they been in? Had Aladar been in that camp? Had they seen him? Heard of him? Was there any news of their husband and father?

Then came the day when they heard, the day when one of the returning Jewish prisoners said, 'Yes, I remember Aladar Kalafoni. He was with me in the Günskirchen concentration camp.'

Kitty and Ada waited for him to say more. His face became solemn. He looked down at his shoes, as if to avoid their eyes, then he slowly shook his head. Ada began to cry, Kitty felt her eyes fill with hot tears, but held them back and asked, 'What happened? How did he die?'

'He had typhus. He was very ill. He had been dying by inches for some time. He died one day after the Americans liberated the camp.'

Kitty and Ada went back to their apartment and wept. They were still crying when Anatole arrived back from his day at the

Red Army headquarters. He was distressed to see them so upset. They managed to explain what had happened. When he finally understood his soft eyes filled with tears, he put his big, beefy arms gently around the two women, and wept with them.

When the tears were finally over Ada said bitterly to Kitty, 'I will never forgive the Nazis for what they have done... *never.*'

'I know, Mama, I know,' murmured Kitty. Again that word sounded in her head: 'Unforgivable!' The pain, the suffering, the hurt that had been inflicted on millions—not as a mass, but as individuals, as families—was, Kitty firmly believed, utterly unforgivable. She was certain that she, at least, would never forgive and never forget. For a moment the face of the megalomaniac who had started it all flashed upon her inward eye—the face she had seen so clearly all those years before.

Over the days and weeks that followed news came in of their other relatives.

Aladar's brother, Alexander, had survived much of the war working as an engraver for Oskar Schindler. Like all of "Schindler's Jews" he was properly fed and well cared for. One day he left Schindler's Brunnlitz factory on an errand. Two SS officers stopped him, and asked him why he looked so well— he was far too well fed and healthy for a Jew, they sneered. And they shot him on the spot.

Aladar's mother, Juliana, had been picked up in the Nazi sweep of Kosice and herded into the cattle wagons that were to take them to the death camps. Juliana, Kitty's grandmother, was an old woman and she did not survive the journey to the camp: she died in the wagon. Her unmarried daughter Margaret also died in the cattle wagon on the way to the death camps.

Kitty's 19-year-old cousin Paul was also transported to the concentration camps. He survived the journey, but he was nursing a broken leg from a sporting accident. When he arrived at Auschwitz, the camp doctor, Dr Joseph Mengle, took one look at his broken leg and ordered him straight into the gas chambers.

When Adolf Hitler's "final solution to the Jewish question" was over, more of Kitty and Ada's family were dead than alive.

24

FOR THE MOMENT, for Kitty and Ada, their immediate problem remained—Tibor. He showed no intention of leaving their apartment, and still talked of marrying Kitty. He was a nice enough man, he had saved Kitty's life in those last days of the war, and she was grateful. How could she be unkind to him?

Then Tibor announced that, because of his communist party connections, he had been appointed head of the police station covering the Lipótváros district. He was clearly becoming a powerful man. This made Kitty even more nervous about saying she didn't want to marry him, and both women more nervous than ever about simply asking him to leave the apartment.

Then, one day, Ada returned from visiting a friend.

'Is Tibor here?' she asked Kitty.

'No, he's out on his police work. Why?'

'I have an idea—an empty apartment.'

'What apartment?'

'Dr Nagy's. Remember, I told you. He died in one of the camps. And he had no family. Someone told me today his apartment is still empty. Do you think Tibor would be interested?'

'We must persuade him,' replied Kitty firmly.

That evening when Tibor returned, the two women sat him

down and told him about the empty apartment. He looked doubtful at first.

'With your new position,' said Kitty, 'and your new responsibilities you really should have your own apartment.'

Tibor swelled a little with self-importance and nodded in agreement.

'And there are so few apartments,' Kitty continued. 'Until they start building work, and that may not be for months, there will continue to be very few places that become available.'

'But we have heard of one,' said Ada, taking up the story. 'Would you like to see it before someone else gets their hands on it?'

The idea of beating others to the mark appealed to Tibor, and it was agreed that the women would take him to Dr Nagy's old apartment, only a few blocks away in Zrínyi Street, the next day.

Tibor strutted around the empty apartment, hands clasped behind his back, with evident pleasure.

'He was a doctor?' he asked. 'The man who used to live here?'

'Dr Nagy,' explained Ada. 'He was a gynaecologist.'

After a long silence Tibor announced, 'It will suit me very well. And it is in my police district. It is suitable accommodation for the police chief of Lipótváros.'

'You'll have to move in quickly,' urged Kitty, 'or someone else will claim it.'

It was arranged that Tibor would move in immediately, that afternoon.

With Tibor out of the apartment, and with his police duties taking more and more of his time, Kitty gradually saw less and less of him. As he became absorbed by his career, and his ambitions, his demand that Kitty would have to marry him slowly faded. Which was how the Tibor problem was solved: not with a bang, but a whimper.

In those early months immediately after the war ended Kitty remained extremely bitter.

Ada walked into the bathroom one morning to see tears streaming down Kitty's face.

'Oh, my pet,' said Ada, 'whatever's wrong? What are you so sad about?'

'I'm not sad,' replied Kitty, wiping away the tears with some embarrassment. 'I'm angry. So many people have done so many, many wicked things. And Papa is dead, and so many...'

She stopped and wiped her eyes again.

'I'm just angry,' she repeated quietly. 'Very, very angry. The people who did these things should hurt...they should die.'

Not long after hearing about the death of her father, Kitty opened the newspaper one morning to read that a group of men had been convicted in the Budapest court the day before of being collaborators with the Nazis. Many of those convicted had been organizers of the slave labour system. They had been sentenced to death, and were to be executed the following morning—shot by firing squads, in the courtyard of the prison.

After they had been shot, their dead bodies, said the newspaper, would be hung from lampposts in one of the main city squares in Budapest.

The following day Kitty walked down to see the bodies.

The square was filled with people, but it was a strangely quiet crowd. They moved in small groups of twos and threes around the square, looking up at the lifeless faces of the convicted men, hanging from the lampposts.

'Good,' said Kitty to herself, 'good. At least some of them have paid.'

'I knew this one,' said a stranger standing beside her—a young woman, about her own age. 'I knew him. He was a member of the *Nyilas* party. And before that he ran one of the slave labour gangs.'

'Death is too good for them,' muttered Kitty.

'Yes,' said the stranger in a quiet, flat voice, devoid of all emotion. 'They should have been put into slave labour gangs themselves—and driven, and driven, and driven...until they died.'

Kitty said nothing, but nodded her head in agreement.

A long silence followed, and then the stranger said, 'Why did you come?'

Kitty shrugged her shoulders, and then said, 'I just had to see. I had to know that at least some of them were caught.'

It was good, she thought to herself, good to know that at least some of the men who had caused such suffering (including her own father's suffering) had paid with their lives. She saw their lifeless bodies suspended above the pavement with a grim satisfaction.

The stranger broke into Kitty's thoughts by asking, 'Did they admit their crimes? Did they ask for mercy?'

'Not according to the newspapers.'

'So they died still not knowing what they did to us.'

'Oh, they knew,' Kitty insisted. 'They must have known. And they enjoyed what they did.'

The young stranger shook her head, whether sadly or in disbelief Kitty couldn't tell, as she muttered, 'Unforgivable.'

Kitty agreed.

'Unforgivable' was her judgement on everything that had happened, and on everyone who had been involved in those events, even in the smallest capacity.

She walked on to the next lamppost with its grim burden. Standing there, alone, she reached out and touched the boots on the dangling body.

An old Jewish man, with wire-framed spectacles came to a halt beside her and looked up. He asked, 'Why did you do that?'

'Do what?'

'Touch his boots.'

'I wanted to be sure. If I touch I am sure.'

She wanted to be sure that people had really paid with their lives for the horror she and millions of others had lived through. Just for a moment she felt the pleasure of revenge, almost like a surge of electricity, but as she walked back towards the apartment the bitterness returned. It wasn't enough. A few men had paid, others had escaped, many had not been caught—it wasn't enough.

25

LIFE IN HUNGARY SLOWLY returned to normal, or, at least, to something a little more normal than wartime conditions.

Elections were held in November 1945. Early the next year, Hungary was declared a republic. After the November elections, a coalition government was formed. The new government introduced many social and economic reforms, including land distribution among the peasants. The coalition consisted of the Smallholder, Social Democratic, Communist, and National Peasant parties. The Smallholders had won a clear majority of the votes in the election. However, the communists gradually gained control of the government, largely because of the continued presence of Soviet troops.

Elections were held again in 1947, and the Communist Party again failed to win a majority of the votes. But by then, they held enough key government posts to extend their control over the country. They banned all opposition parties and, in 1949, gave

Hungary a constitution patterned on that of the Soviet Union.

Matthias Rakosi, head of the Communist Party and head of the Hungarian government, ruled as a dictator.

But the communist years still lay ahead as Kitty and Ada faced the question of how they were to support themselves in the post-war chaos which was the shattered Hungarian economy. Kitty realised that with her father dead, she would have to take responsibility for bringing in an income and caring for her mother. The only real economic activity seemed to be the black market, and so it was to the black market that Kitty looked for an opportunity to earn some money.

Once again their old family friends Joseph and Irma Benes came to their rescue. Joseph Benes was the General Manager of the Hungaria Chemical Factory which was resuming operations as the shattered economy began to function again. He suggested that he would supply Kitty with chemicals used in soap making, and Kitty could sell these to the small soap factories that were springing up. He would, he said, in that tightly regulated market, arrange for Kitty to get an allocated quota so that she could buy supplies of chemicals.

An uncle of Kitty's, Paul Kalotai, was also re-opening the chemical factory he worked for at that time, and offered to sell her industrial chemicals to help support Kitty and Ada.

The cash economy was weak, and a great deal of trade was working on the barter system at the end of the war in 1945. Kitty would take supplies of ammonia and other chemicals to the soap factories—often little more than one room operations—and they would pay for the chemicals by giving her bulk supplies of soap. This soap Kitty could then sell to the National Bank of Hungary. The bank was paying many workers with flour, soap, sugar, and fat, rather than money.

The bank paid in newly minted Hungarian forints—such an unstable currency that Kitty would immediately exchange the forints on the black market for American dollars.

Slowly Kitty and Ada recovered, outwardly at least, from the horrors, the suffering and the loss that had been their experience of the war. They came to terms with the loss of their husband and father. The city of Budapest too began to recover. Bombed out ruins were either pulled down or rebuilt. One by one the old businesses, services and institutions of the city reopened. A new political order, dominated by the communists, slowly crept into place.

Many battalions of the Red Army pulled out and returned to Russia—including Anatole, from whom Kitty and Ada parted sadly, although they were happy for him. Anatole was excited to be going home to his family. But the Russian Army never entirely disappeared, and Hungarians had to get used to the idea that Russia now had a permanent military base on their soil.

As 1946 turned into 1947 Kitty and Ada became settled in their new routine, with Kitty as the breadwinner. With money coming in they could get their apartment repaired and back to something of its former comfort. And they hired a new maid. Veronica was pleased to find a place in domestic service since this meant she was provided with accommodation in a city where most of the buildings had been destroyed by the years of bombing.

During her rounds as a chemical wholesaler Kitty came across an old school friend, a girl named Eva Zwebner, who was doing exactly the same thing. In those days the black market seemed to be employing more people than the official economy. This was a fact that did not go unnoticed. In response, the Hungarian police established a special financial squad for the purposes of tracking down and prosecuting black-market dealers.

When Kitty returned to the apartment one evening she found Ada very agitated.

'What's wrong, Mama?' asked Kitty as she took off her overcoat and scarf.

'Have you heard about Eva?' responded Ada.

'No, I've heard nothing. What have you heard?'

'She's been arrested,' announced Ada dramatically.

'What for?' asked Kitty, although she already suspected the answer.

'For operating on the black market, just like you. Oh, Kitty darling, you might be next.'

Kitty did her best to reassure her mother that all would be well. Which was difficult, since she was not quite convinced of this herself. If the police would bother to track down such a small operator as Eva, then they might track her down too. And what if Eva talked to them and provided information about others in the black market?

Two nights later, on November 25, 1947, there was a knock on the front door. Kitty opened it and saw two men in black raincoats standing on the doorstep. Without asking, she knew they were police officers.

One of them flashed an identification badge, and then said, 'We'd like to ask you some questions about your "activities" Miss Kalafoni.'

Kitty stood back to allow them to enter, but they made no move to come inside.

'Not here,' said the taller of the two men. 'Down at the police station. We'd like you to get your coat and come with us please.'

Kitty found Ada, who was giving instructions to the maid in the kitchen.

'The police!' cried Ada in alarm. 'I knew it would come to this. As soon as that Eva woman was arrested, I knew it would come. She's told them all about you.'

'Perhaps,' said Kitty. 'We can't know that. I have to go with them. You should telephone Joseph Benes—he will know what to do, he will help us.'

Kitty was escorted not to a local police station, but to a central station in the heart of the city. Here she was formally charged and told that she would be held in a cell overnight and interviewed the next day. Everything happened so quickly that it left Kitty feeling dazed. Before she knew what had happened she had left her warm apartment, with the smell of supper cooking, and was being marched down tiled concrete stairs by a custody officer, and locked in a small cell, with only two hard wooden bunks and two blankets, that was already occupied by half a dozen or more other women—gypsies, prostitutes and pick-pockets.

After sitting in the cell, sunk in deep depression for an hour, there came the sound of keys rattling and bolts clanking, and the cell door swung open. In the doorway, standing beside the custody officer, was Veronica, the maid.

'I've brought down your supper, miss,' she said in her small voice. 'I didn't like to think of you missing out on your supper.'

'That's very kind of you, Veronica, thank you,' said Kitty, as she accepted the tray. To the wide-eyed women behind her Kitty explained, 'That's Veronica, our maid.'

As the custody officer pushed the cell door closed one of the prostitutes called out in a raucous voice, 'I'm expecting my butler any minute, send him straight down to the cell please.'

But the laughter and the snide remarks ended when Kitty shared her hot supper with the other inmates.

Two grim, uncomfortable days passed for Kitty as other women came and went from the cell, but there was no news of her case. Then on the third day she was marched upstairs to an interview room.

She was questioned for several hours by the same two officers who had arrested her several nights earlier. Kitty decided that the best defence would be to volunteer nothing, and say as little as possible in response to their questions. This tactic, undoubtedly, made the interview drag out for longer, but it didn't bother Kitty—it was a relief to spend time out of that crowded cell.

That night her period began and Kitty began to feel ill. This gave her an idea—if she was sick, really sick, they would have to take her out of that cell, and perhaps put her in hospital.

She began to call out loudly for the guard. When the cell door opened she doubled up, as if in pain, and groaned convincingly.

'I'm sick,' she moaned. 'Terribly sick. I'm in pain. I need to see a doctor.'

The guard took her upstairs to the custody officer who asked her to describe her symptoms. Kitty doubled over, held her side, and whimpered convincingly.

'Get her off to hospital. I don't want a prisoner to die on me—I'd have hundreds of forms to fill in. Call an ambulance, and let the hospital worry about whether she'll die or not.'

The young man made the phone call and returned to say that an ambulance was on its way. The guard was instructed by the custody officer to stay at Kitty's side at all times.

'If she has to stay in the hospital I'll send somebody to relieve you in a few hours.'

Kitty kept up the act, being careful not to overact, as she was bundled into the ambulance and driven to Rokus Hospital.

As she was taken away Kitty pleaded with the sergeant behind the desk to ring her mother, and tell her where she was being taken.

On being told that her daughter was seriously ill Ada immediately phoned their old family friend Joseph Benes. In his turn Benes pulled some strings to ensure that Kitty would have a private room at the hospital and would see the best doctor available.

The following morning Kitty found an older man, with a

kindly face, in a white coat standing beside her bed.

'I am Dr Rubányi. Your friend, Mr Benes, has arranged for me to look after your case, Miss Kalafoni,' he said, loudly enough for the police guard at the door to hear. Then he sat on the edge of the bed and spoke more quietly.

A few questions were enough to make it clear that Kitty was not really ill.

'But we can't let you go back to that cell,' said the doctor softly. 'At least not yet. I think you'd better have appendicitis. I can quite safely remove a healthy appendix. You will have to stay here at least a week to recover, and that will give Mr Benes time for some legal manoeuvres. He insists that only the best is good enough for the daughter of his old friend.'

The surgery was scheduled for first thing the following morning.

In the afternoon, as Kitty lay in her bed, still recovering from the anaesthetic, Dr Rubányi paid another visit.

'I have good news for you, Miss Kalafoni,' he said, 'perhaps

Joseph and Irma Benes.

slightly surprising news.'

Kitty asked him to explain.

In a soft voice that could not be heard by the police guard the doctor said, 'That perfectly healthy appendix of yours that I removed—it turned out to be diseased after all. It would have started to give you trouble fairly soon anyway. All we've done is to catch it early. And while I was in there I discovered a cyst on one of your ovaries, and I've removed that as well. That's why the incision is so large. But it also justifies us keeping you in hospital a little longer.'

The doctor ordered Kitty to spend the next ten days in hospital recovering from the surgery. The one thought that constantly hovered over Kitty's mind was: after the compulsory recovery period, what would happen? Would she be returned to that cell? Would she be sent to some other prison? Would she go straight from the hospital to a magistrate's court?

On the fourth day of her time in hospital Kitty was visited by a uniformed police officer, who first dismissed the constable on guard duty at the door, and then said, 'When you've recovered Miss Kalafoni, you can go home. We'll be taking no more action against you. We don't have sufficient evidence, so we won't be proceeding against you.'

When the ten days were up, Kitty returned home to continue her recuperation.

The first thing she did when she was fully recovered was go down to the relevant government department to stand in queues, to fill in forms, and then stand in even longer queues, with the aim of becoming a legally registered chemical wholesaler.

And it happened. Once she had the piece of paper in her hand she knew that she was safe from further police prosecution.

And then, Géza Seidl entered Kitty's life.

26

KITTY FIRST MET Géza Seidl at the Hungaria Chemical
Company. When the arrangements for the supply of chemicals for
resale were first made Joseph Benes had said to Kitty, 'There's
a good looking young man you should meet. He's the company
secretary, and he'll be the one you deal with each week.'

Seidl was indeed a good looking young man, and it was soon
clear that he enjoyed Kitty's company.

When they first met, Seidl was the company's golden haired
boy. In those first days and weeks after the war ended, as the
company struggled to get back on its feet and resume production, it was discovered that their entire platinum supply was
missing—looted by the Germans.

However, the Germans had not managed to get all of their
loot out of the country, and there was a possibility that the platinum was still in Hungary somewhere, possibly still in
Budapest. So the hunt was on.

Platinum is a precious, silver-white metal with many special
characteristics. It does not corrode or tarnish when exposed to
air, because it does not combine readily with oxygen or sulphur
compounds found in air. Strong acids that dissolve most met-
als do not attack platinum. Chemical laboratories often use
platinum containers because the metal resists heat and chemicals. And platinum serves as an effective catalyst, a substance
that speeds up chemical reactions. At the Hungaria Chemical
Company it was used as a catalyst in the making of acetic acid
and nitric acid.

Géza Seidl began making quiet inquiries among some locals
he thought might have been involved in helping the Germans
move their looted treasures. All these inquiries pointed towards

the castle district, centred around the royal palace, on the western, or Buda, side of the Danube.

The first castle on the hill overlooking the river had been built by King Béla IV in the 13th century. In the 15th century a Gothic Royal Palace was built on the site, but it was rebuilt in the Renaissance style by King Mátyás in 1458. After the Turkish occupation it was razed and reborn on a smaller scale. Maria Theresa further developed the palace, and it was completed in its modern form in 1905. The Germans had used it as a command centre during their occupation of Budapest.

Géza knew he was looking in the right place when some of the artworks looted by the Germans were found in the palace. Eventually he stumbled on the stolen platinum supply in the palace dungeons—and suddenly he was the hero of the hour. He was offered his choice of reward: either money or a car. He chose the car—a new BMW. He knew that even in the restrictions of post-war Budapest he could always obtain petrol through the company.

It was in his new car that Géza Seidl took Kitty out to dinner.

Seidl was an ambitious entrepreneur who saw no future for himself in a Hungary dominated by the communists, and he began to suggest to Kitty that the two of them should flee the country.

At first Kitty was not interested—Budapest was her home. However, after her brush with the police over black market trading, she began to consider Géza's suggestion seriously.

By 1948 "an Iron Curtain had descended across Europe" (in Winston Churchill's famous phrase). On one side were the democracies of western Europe, while on the other were the communist lands—those countries that had become "satellites" of the Soviet Union, and were caught up in its isolationist policy involving trade barriers, rigid censorship and tight restrictions on the movement of people. Behind the Iron Curtain were

Hungary—and Kitty Kalafoni.

One incident in particular persuaded Kitty that Géza was right, and that it was indeed time to flee to freedom.

In their block of apartments in Academia Street, a minister in the post-war government also lived. His name was Sárkány and he was the State Secretary for the Army in the coalition government. His apartment was around a corner in the corridor from Kitty's apartment—and he shared his accommodation with a young woman named Elizabeth, who was also his secretary at the ministry.

Whenever Kitty met Elizabeth and they talked about Sárkány it was clear to Kitty that Elizabeth was very much in love.

'I know there's a great difference in our ages,' Elizabeth would say, 'but he's so distinguished, and handsome, and he's so attentive to me.'

A few months later the two of them were married.

One night in 1948 there was the sound of heavy military boots tramping up the stairs of the apartment block, and loud hammering on the door of one of the apartments. Kitty opened her front door a few inches and looked out in time to see Sárkány being marched away by Russian soldiers. Young Elizabeth was howling and sobbing. Kitty tried to comfort her but Elizabeth just kept on wailing, 'I'll never see him again. They've got him now—he'll never come back.'

The next day she came to Kitty's apartment carrying a small parcel—a compact object wrapped up in a piece of cloth.

'Will you look after this for me, please Kitty?' she asked.

'What is it?'

'A gun. A small revolver. It was his. He has owned it for some time. But now I'm afraid the authorities will come back and search our apartment. If they find the gun they will accuse me of being a criminal, perhaps they'll say I'm a Nazi and a war criminal, and...' Her voice trailed away.

'Of course,' Kitty replied. 'I'll look after it for you.'

Kitty didn't even take the gun out of its wrappings, she just put it at the back of a drawer and forgot about it.

Several weeks later there was another knock on Kitty's door late at night. She opened the door to see Elizabeth standing there, in her dressing gown, shivering slightly.

'Come in,' said Kitty. 'Don't stand there shivering.'

'No, no I won't come in. I'm sorry to call so late. I've just come to ask for the... package back.'

It took a moment for Kitty to remember the revolver.

'Come in, and I'll fetch it.'

Elizabeth followed Kitty, tentatively, a few steps into the apartment, and stood very still and watched as Kitty took the revolver, still wrapped in its piece of cloth, out of the drawer where she had locked it for safe keeping.

As Kitty handed it over to the young woman Elizabeth said, 'Thank you,' very quietly, and gave a slightly embarrassed smile. She seemed entirely calm and rational, and Kitty never suspected for a minute that anything was wrong.

Later that same night they were all awoken from their sleep.

Kitty and Ada both woke up startled, but they had been through the war, and knew what a gunshot sounded like.

Pulling on their dressing gowns they stepped out onto the landing. There were already several other people there.

'I'm sure it was a gunshot,' said someone.

'From where?' Ada asked, 'where did it come from?'

Fairly quickly the group worked out that the sound had come from Elizabeth's apartment. They tried her front door, and found it unlocked. One of the men went inside and looked around. He came back and said, 'Don't go in. Her body's in the bedroom. I'll call the authorities.'

'What has she done?' asked Kitty, not wanting to accept the obvious.

The man put his fingers to his temple in the shape of an imaginary gun and pulled the trigger.

'Oh, Mama,' said Kitty, once they had returned to their own apartment 'I should never have returned that gun to her.'

'Don't blame yourself,' Ada replied, 'you weren't to know.'

Kitty knew she was right. But that incident was enough to make up her mind. Under the Nazis Kitty had survived living in one police state—she didn't want to live in another.

She sat down and talked over her feelings with her mother.

'You and Géza should go,' said Ada firmly. 'You go ahead, and I'll follow after you.'

Kitty's uncle, Paul Kalotai was one of the directors of a company that owned a chemical factory in Vienna, as well as one in Budapest. Géza Seidl had met Kalotai through Kitty, and had the idea that if he could persuade "Uncle Paul" to appoint him to the Vienna factory he could leave the country legally.

'It will be safer and easier if we leave separately,' Géza told Kitty. 'Travelling together would only double our risk of being stopped.'

Géza approached Kitty's uncle with a proposition: he would obtain the Hungaria Chemical Company's formula for a new soap product—a convenient new form of washing powder—and take this to Vienna to be put into production for sale in those western European countries that the Hungaria company could not export to under the Soviet imposed trade restrictions. This sounded like an excellent business opportunity to Paul Kalotai, and he readily agreed.

Géza did not resign from his job—he simply left on his annual vacation. If he had resigned, word was sure to reach government officials that he had no intention of returning. As it was, his papers were processed by the various government departments whose approval was needed to take a "holiday" in Austria, and he was free to leave. Géza drove from Budapest to Vienna in his

BMW, carrying in the back a suitcase filled with some of Kitty's clothes, and the Kalafoni family silver.

He had, however, one small problem: he had not succeeded in obtaining the formula for the new washing powder, and so, with no training in chemical research Géza set to work in the laboratory of the Vienna chemical plant to develop the new washing powder himself.

Now, it was Kitty's turn to escape.

27

HAVING TALKED THINGS over with her mother, and made her plans, Kitty bid a tearful goodbye to Ada, and to Veronica the maid, and set out by train to the border city of Sopron. Once again Uncle Paul had come to her aid. He had relatives in Sopron and they had promised to help Kitty get across the border.

The train carried Kitty through the hills and mountains of the region called *Transdanubia*. South of the railway line was fertile farmland, and from the window of her railway carriage Kitty could see green countryside rolling past—rich farmlands, with white cottages and farm houses dotted at regular intervals. Occasionally a small dairy farm could be seen, or farmhouses surrounded by pigpens or chicken runs. These small family holdings were in the process of being taken over by the communist government and amalgamated into large state collective farms. The countryside was not a happy place in Hungary in 1948.

The line wound among hills and crossed small rivers. Tall clumps of trees—pointed conifers—would announce the arrival of another town or village, where the train would stop and some passengers would alight while others boarded.

Kitty was excited by the new life opening up before her, sad to be leaving the home of her childhood, and nervous about getting past the border guards.

Most people who tried to escape from the communist regime, across the border into free Europe, did so on foot. Kitty had thought of walking out of the country, but it would involve paying a guide. The asking price was steep—5,000 American dollars—and the guides took their charges through the mountainous regions where there were fewer border guards. The "people smuggling" system was well organized by this time, but Kitty had heard many cautionary tales about this type of escape—incompetent guides, dishonest guides, and the dangers of land mines. So, Kitty decided to try and escape by train.

At last the train reached the foothills of the Austrian Alps, and began to climb towards Sopron. At the railway station Kitty was met by distant relatives, connections of Paul Kalotai. What Kitty needed was a temporary travel visa called a Border Pass. These were issued by the authorities to local peasants who had family members on both sides of the border. Her relatives had arranged things: Kitty would be able to buy a border pass from a local peasant girl for $300.

That night she was taken to a cottage on the outskirts of Sopron and, with barely a word spoken, handed over the money and received in exchange the wallet-sized, passport-like Border Pass. Opening it up Kitty saw that it authorised travel only as far as the first village on the other side of the border, Neunkirchen. She also saw that it contained a photograph of the girl it had been issued to.

Kitty's relative tapped the photograph with a forefinger and said, 'You're going to have to look like that. Do you think you can manage it?'

'Yes,' replied Kitty. 'It's not a very clear photograph, and she's about my age. It shouldn't be difficult.'

The next morning Kitty boarded the train, dressed in scruffy clothes, and with a scarf wound around her head. She could take very little with her on her flight—only what she could carry in one small bag. Clearly it would have been highly suspicious for a peasant girl making a day trip to the next village to be seen carrying a large suitcase.

Kitty sat in a corner of the carriage, and was careful not to talk to anyone—her speech would quickly give her away as not being the peasant she was pretending to be.

The train chuffed and rattled and wheezed its way up the steeper slopes, and, finally, rolled into the first village on the Austrian side of the border, Neunkirchen. Kitty sat very still. This was where her border pass said she was supposed to get off. She waited to see if a conductor, or some other official, would walk through the carriage checking documents, but no one came.

At last, with a great hiss of steam and a clank of couplings, the train resumed its journey—deeper into Austria, towards Vienna, and towards freedom. Now they were travelling through a part of the Austrian Alps called the "Alpine Forelands". Some of the scenery Kitty recognised from those distant days when she had been a schoolgirl in Austria—when life had stretched before her like a sunny adventure, before evil and hateful men had done despicable and unforgivable things to her and millions of others.

Each station, each stop, was a risk, but Kitty sat quietly in her corner and spoke to no one. As the tree clad mountainsides and picturesque villages slipped past the windows of the carriage, Kitty looked steadfastly at the scenery and avoided the gaze of her fellow passengers. Fortunately no one looked twice at the badly dressed peasant girl with the scarf around her head and a nervous expression on her face.

Before long the train was rolling into the great platform at Vienna's Südbahnhof railway station. And there on the platform, waiting for her, was Géza. Beside him was Ili Bátory, a cousin of Kitty's mother, who lived here in Vienna with her husband Nicholas.

'Quite a welcoming committee,' said Kitty as she kissed Géza and hugged Ili.

As Géza asked her about the journey, and talked about his plans, Kitty took a deep breath and looked around: she had escaped from behind the Iron Curtain—but her journey to freedom had only just begun.

The Vienna in which Kitty had arrived was very different from the Vienna she had seen as a schoolgirl. As a result of the terrible fighting at the end of the war, including the air raids and artillery bombardments, almost a quarter of the buildings had been partly or completely destroyed. Almost 87,000 apartments had become uninhabitable, and there were more than 3,000 bomb craters in the city area. The population of Vienna had been reduced by perhaps a third to a little more than one million.

In April of 1945 Vienna had been taken by Soviet troops. In September of that year the city, like Austria as a whole, was divided into four zones of occupation by the Allied powers. This situation was to remain until May 15, 1955 when the signing of the *Austrian State Treaty* led to independence and the withdrawal of all Allied occupation troops.

When Kitty arrived in 1948 Vienna was still occupied by Allied forces, and the city was divided into four zones—the British, American, French and Russian zones. Where these four zones met was an inner-city area called the "Inter-Allied Zone" which was administered by each of the four Allied powers on a rotating basis.

There were military checkpoints between the different zones, and soldiers and military vehicles patrolled the streets. These were often combined patrols based on the "four men in a jeep" principle—one American, one French, one British and one Russian.

Each occupation zone was, for all intents and purposes, economically autonomous, and each was loosely attached to the respective occupation areas in Germany (America and France), Italy (Britain) and Hungary (Russia).

Because of the Cold War tensions that had arisen between Russia and the west, the Russian zone had a distinctive, and more repressive, atmosphere than the other Allied zones. Russia was determined to reap some economic benefit from its occupation of Austria. But it was less interested in interfering politically, and did not support the Austrian communist party in that way in which it had, in effect, provided the muscle that had put the communists into power in Hungary.

28

THE FIRST THING GÉZA and Kitty did was to go to St Michael's church to give thanks for Kitty's safe arrival. Neither would have described themselves as believers of any sort, but the sense of relief, almost of joy, produced by escaping from behind the Iron Curtain was so profound that they felt they just had to thank someone—even if they didn't really know about, or care about, the Someone they were thanking.

It was arranged that, for the time being at least, Kitty would move in with Ili Bátory and her husband Nicholas in their apartment in Stahlburgasse in the American quarter.

First thing the next morning Kitty presented herself to the American authorities to register as a "displaced person". Over the days and weeks that followed she made frequent visits to the American diplomatic office, seeking to be issued with that vital document that would identify her as an officially recognised "displaced person", and, as such, eligible for admission to another country under a refugee program.

Kitty had no money, and Géza very little (his salary at the chemical plant being restricted until he produced the washing powder formula he kept promising). However, he had one asset—the BMW. But petrol was scarce and expensive. Eventually, over a year later, Géza sold the car when he and Kitty began to run short of money to feed and clothe themselves.

Six weeks after arriving Kitty became seriously ill. She had cramps and a searing, burning discomfort that made her almost double over with pain. A concerned Ili took Kitty to her own doctor, who conducted a brief examination and then said, 'Hospital for you, young lady. You have an extremely serious inflammation. You need penicillin for the infection, and anti-inflammatory drugs, and you need hospital care. I'm sending you to the special women's clinic, and they'll want to keep you there for some time.'

Kitty was admitted to a hospital in the American quarter later that day. She spent a total of six weeks in that hospital bed.

After one of the hospital physicians had taken her medical history, Kitty asked, 'What has caused this? How did I come down with it?'

The doctor looked down at the clip-board on which he had been writing and replied, 'This is the culmination of all your wartime experiences. I've seen this sort of thing before. It's the result of long periods of not eating properly, of winters spent shivering with cold, of lowered resistance to viral or bacterial infection. The body can take only so much of that sort of treatment. Did you have no hint, no prior warning, of this inflammatory attack?'

'Back in Budapest,' admitted Kitty, 'I had a slight inflammation once, and my doctor said exactly what you have just said—it was a product of the war years.'

'I see. Well, he was undoubtedly correct, but this time it is serious.'

'How serious?'

'It may mean, and I say only 'may' at this stage, that you will never be able to have children.'

Kitty wept silently into her pillow after he was gone. She had always imagined that one day she would marry and have children. She was very much in love with Géza. She wanted to marry him and have his children. It was the picture she had always had of the future. It was what she wanted. And this too was to be denied to her. One more thing the Nazis had done to her—one more thing to be angry and bitter about.

Later, when Ili and Nicholas Bátory came to visit her, she

didn't tell them the news. Instead, she tried to put on a bright face, and arranged for them to sell some of her family's silver cutlery to pay her medical bills.

Towards the end of her stay Kitty was visited by the young ward doctor accompanied by an older, distinguished looking man.

'This is Professor Antoine,' said the young physician. 'He is professor of gynaecology, the leader in his field.'

Professor Antoine sat on the end of Kitty's bed and spoke gently in a sympathetic voice.

'I have looked at your medical records, Miss Kalafoni,' he explained, 'and examined the results of the tests. I hate having to break this sort of news to a young woman, but I am afraid, Miss Kalafoni, that you will never have children.'

Again that night, when she was alone, Kitty wept. And then buried the bitterness deep in her heart. But she told no one about what the doctors had said. In due course, the inflammation cleared up, the pain went away, and Kitty was released. She went back to Stahlburgasse, and the spare room she had in the Bátory's apartment.

Géza remained optimistic about the washing powder he was researching. He had succeeded in communicating his enthusiasm to others, and had persuaded the chemical plant to spend a good deal of money on equipment and supplies for the laboratory where he was working. The problem was that he was no chemist, and lacked the technical expertise to achieve his goal. In time, Paul Kalotai would grow impatient, becoming irritable and suspicious of the amount of money being spent without success, and would start firing off terse angry notes demanding reports, and, more than reports—results.

But that was all ahead, and, for the time being Kitty and Géza were together and that was all they cared about.

America was the first place they dreamed of going together. Kitty began the long, slow process of applying for admission to the United States as a refugee. This involved filling in forms, attending interviews, undergoing medical examinations, and waiting. Mostly waiting.

Vienna was a grey and depressing city in those years. And to be in Vienna and desperately short of money and with not enough to do to fill the time made the bleak greyness of those long days even worse. It was having nothing to do that led to the feeling of being both hopeless and helpless—aggravated by the knot of bitterness that tied her up inside. The Bátorys were kind and generous, but they too had little money, and Kitty was aware of imposing on them.

Even during the worst days of the war there had, at least, been constant activity, constant danger, a need to stay alert in order to stay alive. Staying alive was no longer a problem. But staying alive was no longer enough. Kitty wanted to see everyone who had ever done anything to hurt her or her family punished. She wanted them to suffer. And she urgently wanted to escape from a bleak and war-ravaged Europe and start again—find work to do, marry, raise a family (perhaps, if the doctors were right, she could adopt). But all there was to do now was wait. And then wait some more.

Life had been drained of its colour and its energy. The world was shades of grey, and everything seemed to move so slowly—especially the hands of the clock on the wall of Kitty's bedroom. When the Bátorys were out of their apartment the place was so quiet—so dead. Kitty had always been a bright, lively, energetic young woman. Forced inactivity was draining her reserves in a way that wartime danger and challenge never had.

And inactivity meant time to think: time to think about the death of her beloved Papa in a Nazi death camp; of all the members of her family who had died under Hitler's "final solution"; of how close she herself had been to death so many times during the war; of the family apartment back in Budapest; of the bad news she had heard from the gynaecologist. She had time to dwell on the frustration she felt because she could do nothing to bring to justice the evil men who had taken away her father and caused so much pain and suffering.

But more than that, she found herself thinking about the future and seeing little or no hope ahead. If power could be in the hands of such evil men once, it could happen again. Kitty was profoundly frightened for the first time in her life. Her nerves had remained tough through the worst days of the war, and the communist take-over that followed, but now she faced leaving the world she had known all her life. She would, most probably, have to travel as a refugee to some remote part of the globe. She would have to start again with absolutely nothing.

The uncertainty of it all weighed more heavily upon her than the immediate dangers of the war had ever done. That's what she could feel: a weight that was dragging her spirits down. It was the heavy burden of an uncertain, insecure future. She tried to look ahead, and could see nothing but bleak fog.

One particular grey afternoon Kitty was alone in the apartment—both the Bátorys were out. It was raining outside, light, misty rain like teardrops. It was cold, and wet and miserable. The greyness seemed to be closing in on Kitty. The last of her energy seemed to have gone, and with it the last of her hope. She looked up and caught sight of her face in a mirror, and was startled to see that she was crying.

She wiped her eyes, and dabbed at her nose, and kept saying to herself, 'This won't do. This just won't do. I'm not this sort of person.' Then, ten minutes later, she found herself sobbing again.

'Sleep,' Kitty thought to herself, 'if I could just have a long sleep I would wake up and feel so much better.'

She began to pace around the small apartment looking for

the sleeping tablets that she knew Ili Bátory kept somewhere.

'Sleep,' thought Kitty, as she opened cupboards and looked in drawers. 'I need a long, relaxing sleep. A soothing sleep. And when I wake up it won't be raining and it won't be cold. I feel so dreadfully, dreadfully tired—if I could just sleep, really sleep, deeply and soundly, then I would be so much better off.'

Kitty found the sleeping tablets and a bottle of brandy to wash them down with. She sat on the side of her bed, poured the brandy into a glass, and used it to wash down a tablet. She waited a few minutes, lying back on the bed with her eyes closed. The tablet didn't seem to be working, so she took another one. Then she had another glass of brandy and walked over to the window to watch the rain falling and the puddles forming in the street. The few pedestrians were huddling under umbrellas or dashing from one covered awning to the next.

She lay down on her bed and stared at the ceiling. Sleep wasn't coming, the sleep she so desperately needed, the soothing, healing sleep she longed for. Kitty swallowed another sleeping tablet and another glass of brandy. Perhaps she dozed briefly, but she didn't fall properly, deeply asleep. With an effort Kitty pushed herself up off the bed and walked over to the mirror. She was horrified at the bleak emptiness she saw, and the tears that were forming again in her eyes. And she knew that buried somewhere, deeply, behind those hollow, empty eyes was an unforgiving bitterness.

Perhaps one more sleeping tablet would do the trick? How many sleeping tablets had she taken? She couldn't remember, her mind was becoming cloudy, but, somehow, she was certain she had only taken one. A second one couldn't hurt, could it? Kitty poured out another glass of brandy with a shaky hand and swallowed another tablet.

Kitty was feeling more confused than ever now, but not

properly sleepy, not really. And it was sleep she was longing for. She lay on the bed and took another tablet, convinced, once again, that it was only the second and couldn't do any harm.

Finally sleep came, but not soothing sleep—a restless, uncomfortable, hot, twisting and turning sleep.

The next thing Kitty knew Ili was standing over her screaming and shaking her shoulders. Ili's husband Nicholas was pounding down the stairs shouting, 'I'll telephone for an ambulance'.

Ili was forcing Kitty onto her feet, saying, 'You must walk—move around—wake up—'

'But I'm tired,' mumbled Kitty. 'Just let me sleep...all I need is a good sleep...I'll feel so much better if I can only sleep...'

'No—you mustn't sleep! Stay awake.'

Then there were ambulance men, and a stretcher, and a ride in the ambulance.

She was moved and bounced around on a stretcher and then a trolley. People shouted at her, and she tried to answer. They did things to her that she didn't like to remember afterwards—especially having her stomach pumped. After that she slept. Finally, exhausted by all that had happened, she slept deeply for hours and hours.

She awoke to find herself in a hospital bed.

'Where am I?' she asked, when a white jacketed doctor entered the room.

'You are in the psychiatric hospital, my dear.'

'But why?'

'You tried to take your own life. You attempted to commit suicide.'

'No, no,' protested Kitty. 'This is some sort of mistake.'

'You consumed a handful of sleeping tablets, and half a

dozen glasses of brandy—are you telling me that was a mistake?'

Kitty put a hand to her head which was now throbbing painfully.

'My memory's not awfully clear,' she confessed. 'But I'm certain I never intended to die. I just wanted to sleep.'

'I see,' the doctor muttered doubtfully as he made a note. 'We'll keep you in here for a few days and keep an eye on you, shall we?'

He sounded patronising and superior and Kitty began to feel irritated.

Taking a deep breath Kitty said calmly, 'There's been a mistake. I did not attempt suicide and, apart from this headache, I'm now feeling fine, and I would like to go home.'

'Tomorrow. Perhaps. We'll see,' said the doctor, as he left the room, locking the door behind him.

Over the next few days Kitty had the opportunity to see, at first hand, the genuinely mentally ill. She felt great pity for them, but the more she saw of them the more certain she was that she had to get out of that place.

As the days passed the doctors began to see that Kitty was a stable, confident and normal young woman, and they began to accept her story that the incident was an accident, not a suicide attempt. Géza came to visit her and joined in her efforts to get the doctors to see sense.

Eventually the medical authorities agreed and Kitty was released. The Bátorys came and signed for her, and took her back to their apartment. And, at her insistence, her admission was not recorded as "attempted suicide". Such a note on her medical record would be certain to bar her from entry to America as a refugee.

But there was already one black cloud on that horizon.

When the American medical authorities X-rayed her for

tuberculosis they had discovered a small spot on her lung, and that might just be enough to close the doors on migration to the United States. So, if not America, where else was there to go? Where else might take her and Géza? Where else might they find a new life?

29

 AMONG THE MAIDS THE Kalafonis had employed over the years, the one who had stayed longest was Emma. She had come to them after being maid to a leading operatic soprano, Alpar Gitta, and she had stayed for 20 years. Over that time a closeness, and real friendship, had grown up between Ada and Emma. Emma had given Ada the nickname of "Dalai Lama" (for reasons she never explained), and Ada allowed Emma to borrow her fur coat to wear to the opera. Emma was almost one of the family.

And when, in 1949, Ada decided to escape from Hungary it was to Emma that she turned for help. Emma was by this time retired and living in the small village of Kazincbarcika, her home town, in the north east of the country, near the Czechoslovakian border.

Ada packed a small bag with those essentials she could take with her on a difficult journey (including such cash and jewellery as she still had), locked up the family apartment in Academia Street for the last time, and took a tram down to the railway station. She travelled by train from Budapest to Kazincbarcika, where she stayed with Emma for several days, while Emma made inquiries about possible guides to lead Ada over the border.

Eventually the arrangements were made, money changed hands, Ada and Emma said farewell, and Ada walked, with the guide she was paying, over the border into Czechoslovakia. The guide took her through steep, hilly country as far as the village of Safárikovo. Once there, Ada caught a train to Bratislava, in the east of Czechoslovakia, close to the Austrian border. There she went to an address her guide had given her, and found another man who was part of the "people smuggling" black market. For a fee he agreed to walk her over the border and into Austria. This last leg of her journey she found difficult and tiring, even though she was still a relatively young woman—only 49 years of age.

Ada arrived in Vienna with almost nothing. The cash and jewellery had been spent paying for the guides, and her bag had gradually been emptied as she left behind anything too heavy to carry in that last, exhausting leg of her journey.

In Vienna there was a welcome reunion between mother and daughter. Ada complained about her feet after all that walking, and told the story of her escape.

'And what about you?' asked Ada. 'What has been happening to you since you arrived in Vienna?'

'Well, I've been to the American consulate I don't know how many times, filling in forms and being interviewed. And I've been in hospital twice...'

'Hospital? What happened? What was wrong?'

Kitty told Ada the full story, and, at that point, Ada decided that she needed to take over.

Immediately Ada began visiting people she knew in Vienna—distant relatives, friends of friends, members of Jewish refugee organizations and local rabbis.

Kitty, meanwhile, was looking for an apartment large enough to share with Ada. She found one and moved in, but after only a week, decided it was too expensive. That was when Ada came up with a solution to the problem of low cost accommodation,

'It's all fixed,' she announced. 'I've arranged for us to move into the Rothschild Hospital.'

'A hospital?' asked Kitty.

'It's not a hospital any longer,' Ada explained. 'It's been converted into a Jewish refugee hostel. And I've arranged that we shall share a room—just the two of us, a room to ourselves.'

So Kitty and Ada moved into the Rothchilds Jewish Refugee

Camp—as it was officially known. There they were provided with basic meals, and given a small weekly cash allowance.

Knowing that inactivity was not good for Kitty, and that the two women needed money, Nicholas Bátory introduced Kitty to a friend, a Jewish garment manufacturer who had just reopened his factory after the devastation of the war years.

'All he's making at the moment,' explained Nicholas, 'is scarves—printed scarves. But they're beautiful products and he needs someone to act as his representative—to take samples to the shops and take their orders.'

And so Kitty spent much of each day visiting clothing shops, showing sample scarves and taking orders. This additional money enabled them to supplement their meagre diet with more, and better, food, often from the black market.

One morning, as she was walking from one shop to the next with her sample scarves, Kitty saw an old friend she had known in Budapest. His name was Stephen Kondor, and he introduced Kitty to the young woman he was with, Lívia Simon—his fiancée. They made arrangements to meet again, and, over the weeks and months that followed, they became good friends. The four of them, Géza and Kitty and Stephen and Lívia, would often go out together—perhaps to one of Vienna's famous coffee houses that were slowly coming back into business as the old life of the city was resumed.

Kitty and Lívia, in particular, became close friends.

As 1950 dawned, the process of applying for permission to enter the United States as a refugee dragged on and on. Whenever Kitty inquired she would be told, 'We have to thoroughly investigate the background of everyone who wants to enter the United States, and, in your case, we're still investigating.'

The process was one of constant delay. Kitty began to suspect that they had been so thorough in their investigations they had found out about her short stay at the hospital. And so she decided to apply elsewhere, while the Americans continued their endless inquiries.

She talked to the others about this, and, after much debate and discussion, the general consensus was that Australia looked like a good option. Lívia became particularly enthusiastic about this idea. So, Kitty and Lívia went together to the Australian consulate in Vienna to apply for permission to go to Australia as refugees.

At the Australian consulate there were forms to be filled in— many forms, in triplicate—and a long series of interviews. And they began the process of conducting preliminary medical examinations of the two young women.

At length they were issued with documents by the consulate: each received a *Certificate of Identity for the Purpose of Immigration to Australia*. This certificate took the place of the passport that Kitty and Lívia, as refugees, did not have. Since Hungary would not provide passports for any of its citizens who escaped as refugees, this substitute certificate was issued under the authority of an international body called the IRO—the International Refugee Organization.

Kitty was finally issued with her certificate on March 1, 1951. It identified her as Displaced Person number 1,009,627 and was stamped and authorised by the Australian Military Mission in Germany.

There were three centres at which refugee applicants for Australia were processed: Vienna, Salzburg and Hamburg. The most important of these three centres was Salzburg, a much smaller city than Vienna (perhaps a tenth of its size) located in the mountains of north-western Austria.

The next steps in the process would happen in Salzburg. 'Our consulate there,' the offical explained, 'is the main clearing centre for European refugees, so you'll have to go there for your applications to be processed. There is another refugee camp in

Salzburg, and we can arrange accommodation for you there.'

So, Kitty and Lívia moved to Salzburg to spend their days filling in more forms at the Australian consulate there, being interviewed at length, and undergoing more medical testing. Kitty's mother Ada remained in Vienna, where she was applying to the Australian consulate for a refugee travel visa.

Géza had a friend from Hungary who was living in Melbourne, and so wrote to him and asked for a letter saying that he would act as sponsor and guarantor for him in the migration process. Stephen had found a similar sponsor for himself. Not having sponsors, Kitty and Lívia had to sign work agreements for the Australian refugee authorities.

'We'll see you in Australia,' Géza said, as they parted from the two young women, 'and we'll see who gets there first—you or us.'

30

AT THE AUSTRALIAN consulate in Salzburg the whole process began again from, so it seemed, the very beginning.

There were forms to be filled in, many forms, again in triplicate. Kitty and Lívia were interviewed—not just once, but many times. Then there was a series of tests they had to undertake—written exams designed to test aptitude, character, language skills, political understanding, political background, and much more besides. The interviews often focussed on questions such as: why had she left Budapest? What work was she trained to do? What sort of work was she prepared to accept? The questions just went on and on.

And then there were the medicals.

When Kitty and Lívia met on the footpath in front of the Australian consulate after one of these medical examinations, Kitty said, 'I feel like a horse someone is thinking of buying. They looked at my teeth, my muscles—at everything.'

'What worries me,' Lívia responded, 'are the X-rays. They are concerned about TB and they keep looking for spots on the lung. But just about everyone in Europe has a spot on the lung somewhere. You don't think this will keep us out of Australia, do you?'

When they returned to the consulate for their next appointment there was yet another medical examination—this time looking at physical stamina. The women were told to lift up a wooden office chair—from the floor to head height and down again—as often as they could, while a clerk kept count.

Both before and after this exercise the consulate's doctor came in with his stethoscope to measure their heart rate.

Blood samples were taken for testing, and a second lot of X-rays required. On and on went the tests. And in between the medical tests were more interviews to test their suitability for refugee status, and their suitability as migrants.

In Salzburg there was a casino. After long weeks in a dreary refugee camp Kitty and Lydia decided to put on their best dresses and go out for a night at the casino. But no sooner had they arrived when they were horrified to see the Australian consular official who had interviewed them. Realising that their presence might not create the right impression, they turned around and promptly left again.

Ada had already decided that she didn't want to travel immediately to Australia with Kitty (she was worried Kitty might not like Australia and may simply want to leave again). But Ada was to follow Kitty to Australia a year later, where she eventually re-married—to an Austrian man she met in Australia.

From Salzburg Kitty and Lívia moved on to Hamburg—Germany's second largest city and one of the largest seaports in Europe. It was from here that the refugee ships departed for Australia.

The two young women were in Hamburg for only a few days, during which time they were X-rayed again to ensure that they didn't have TB. Eventually the long bureaucratic process came to an end, visas were issued, and Kitty and Lívia were given a departure date. They wrote to Géza and Stephen with the news, and Kitty also wrote to her mother.

And it came: departure day.

At busy Bremen harbour they boarded the ocean liner *Fairsea* which had been chartered to carry European refugees to Australia. The *Fairsea* had spent the Second World War as a troop transport, and although it was now returning to civilian service, and had been chartered as a refugee ship, it was still fitted out as a troop ship. In place of individual cabins, the accommodation space on the ship was divided into large dormitory-style sleeping areas. Hundreds of people slept together in row upon row of army cots. Most of the refugees, Kitty discovered, were not from eastern or middle Europe, but from southern Europe, mostly Italy and Greece.

As they looked forward to long weeks at sea both Kitty and Lívia had mixed emotions—they were sailing towards Géza and Stephen (who had left a few weeks before on another migrant ship), but they disliked the idea of sleeping in a large, crowded cabin with strangers whose languages they did not share.

However, they made the acquaintance of the ship's doctor. Both were charming and good looking young women, and the doctor enjoyed their company. In particular, it was clear that he enjoyed Lívia's company. When they told him about their concerns, he offered a creative solution to the accommodation issue. The doctor offered to "find" some spots, or other marks of infection, on their bodies and put them into quarantine. In fact, in

Lívia and Kitty with the ship doctor.

order to make his "discovery" more convincing he put red "infection" spots all over their bodies with his red ball-point pen.

Delighted by this plan Lívia and Kitty quickly agreed, and spent the rest of the voyage with their own cabin (the "quarantine" cabin), and even their own deck area where they could walk, and take in the fresh sea air, without "infecting" the other passengers.

The *Fairsea* arrived in Melbourne on April 25—Anzac Day—1951. After six weeks at sea they were disappointed to learn that they would have to spend another day on the boat, because it was a public holiday, and the customs and immigration officers at Port Melbourne were not working.

The next day the ship's passengers streamed through customs and immigration like cattle through a cattle race. And from the customs shed all the new arrivals were herded on board a passenger train that would take them to Bonegilla refugee camp. Some of the Jewish refugees made black jokes about being herded aboard trains and sent to camps—but they knew that this was a passenger train, not a cattle wagon, and they were headed for a very different sort of camp.

On the walls of the railway carriage was a map showing the rail lines of the State of Victoria—and what struck Kitty and Lívia (and the other passengers) were the strange place names: Wangaratta, Yackandandah, Tallangatta, Yarrawonga, Tallarook and Wodonga. And it was Wodonga, they discovered, that was their destination.

There they alighted from the train and transferred to buses for the final leg of the long, hot journey from Melbourne. They arrived that evening at Bonegilla Refugee Camp, a former army camp that consisted of row upon row of tin huts. It looked like an entire village built out of corrugated iron.

Kitty and Lívia were allocated a hut together—the furniture consisting of nothing but a double bunk. Lívia claimed the bottom bunk, and Kitty said she was happy to settle for the top bunk—a decision she was to regret later that night.

Having left their bags in their hut they assembled with the others in a large dining hall for an evening meal.

'Just like all camp food,' complained Lívia, as they walked back to their hut later, 'simply awful.' In fact, the food was the same every day—mutton stew, followed by jelly. The only thing that ever changed was the colour of the jelly: one day it was green, the next yellow, the next red, and then it was back to green again.

'At least we're not starving,' Kitty said philosophically, 'and surely we won't be in this place for very long.'

It was a brilliant moonlit night, with a sharp silvery-blue light picking out every detail of the rows of huts and every leaf in the surrounding gum trees. There were no ceilings in these old army huts, and so, when they retired for the night, Kitty found herself sleeping directly underneath the timber rafters, and the corrugated iron roof.

It had been a busy, bustling day and it took some time for Kitty to fall asleep—her mind kept buzzing with images of this strange new land. Eventually sleep came, but she had not slept for long when she was awoken by an unusual sound. She lay very still in her bed and listened carefully. After a while the silence of the night was broken once again by the noise—a sharp, clattering, scratching noise. It sounded very close. Kitty's eyes raked the roof, where the bright, blue moonlight came through the gaps at the tops of the walls.

Suddenly she froze: a huge, hairy, bushy tail was curling around the edge of the roof and onto the rafter just inches above Kitty's head. She screamed. Lívia woke up with a start, crying, 'What's happened? What's going on?'

Kitty screamed again as she scrambled out of bed.

'Up there,' she said breathlessly, pointing at the rafter. 'Up there!'

Her scream had echoed through the camp, and a moment later one of their neighbours was at the door of their hut, in his pyjamas and dressing gown, and carrying a torch.

'What's happened?' he asked anxiously. 'What's wrong?'

Kitty tried to explain as she pointed at the rafters, but her heart was pounding rapidly and she seemed to be short of breath.

'Just a moment,' said their visitor, as he stepped outside and flashed his torch at the roof of the hut. 'I thought so,' he said, and picked up a small stone from the ground, which he threw at something on the roof. This produced another rattle of the scratching, clattering sound, and then—silence.

The man stood in the doorway of the hut and said solemnly, 'You have just had your first encounter, miss, with an Australian possum.'

Then he nodded his head, switched off his torch and, as he turned to go, said, 'Good night.'

31

AFTER A FEW MONTHS at the camp, Kitty took a job as live-in housekeeper for a wealthy Melbourne family. This was work that she was never cut out for—because she had never learned to cook. A cousin in the family offered to find her an office job, and she was eventually employed by the SKF Ball Bearing Company. Without regret, she said an affectionate farewell to the Elliots.

Kitty was so happy to be away from domestic chores, and in an office, that each morning at work she would put her head down and work without stopping until lunch, and again from lunch until finishing time. After a few days she noticed that the rest of the women in the office were not speaking to her, and seemed upset about something.

Finally, Kitty summoned up enough courage to ask the friendliest of them, 'Why aren't the girls talking to me?'

'Because you never come to the lunch room for morning and afternoon tea. If you keep working when we stop for a cup of tea, you make us look bad.'

From then on Kitty took care to take the morning and afternoon tea breaks with the others, and from then on her relations with the rest of the staff in the office were warm and friendly.

Kitty moved into a boarding house and began enjoying the social life of the city. As well as working by day for CSR, Géza played the piano each night in a café in Collins Street. There was a large circle of European refugees in Melbourne at that time, many of them young, like Géza and Kitty, and these people became the social circle in which they moved.

Géza was living in rooms above a pub in Swanston Street. The previous occupant of the rooms had been the owner of the local pub who had recently died. This man had been (at least by reputation) a millionaire, and when Géza heard some of the floorboards creak he became convinced the man had hidden either money or jewellery under the floor. Following this "discovery" Kitty and Géza spent many of their spare hours pulling up the boards, and searching the cavity beneath. They found nothing.

Kitty's Mother, Ada, arrived in Melbourne in the winter of 1952.

A month of Melbourne's winter weather was enough for Ada.

'This is too cold for me,' she told Kitty. 'During the last months of the war, in the ghetto, I froze. I don't ever want to be cold again. Let's move to Sydney. That will be warmer, and I know a lot of people in Sydney. There's a big Hungarian community there.'

Kitty opened her mouth to protest, but Ada continued, 'Besides which, your relationship with Géza is going nowhere. If you move to Sydney either he'll get serious and follow you there, or else you'll be better off without him.'

Kitty didn't respond immediately. She knew that her relationship with Géza was shaky. He was keen to have children, and, if she was to believe the specialist in Vienna, Kitty could never give him children. She knew that Géza would blame her for the lack of a family, and their relationship would never work. Sooner or later he would resent not having children and heirs—and it would stand as a barrier between them.

Over the next few weeks Kitty decided that Ada was right—she should break off the relationship with Géza and the two of them should move to Sydney.

At the factory Kitty had, at first, done clerical work, but later she had moved into the accounts department and specialised in bookkeeping. The company thought well of her, and when she announced that she wanted to move to Sydney, they found a place for her in their Sydney office.

In Sydney Kitty and Ada settled into a rented apartment in Elizabeth Bay, and began mixing with the large Hungarian expatriate community.

One day, at the Blue Danube Coffee Lounge in Elizabeth Bay Road, Kitty was introduced to Alec Diosy.

'We've met before,' he said, as they shook hands.

'Really?' responded Kitty. 'Where did we meet?'

'In Vienna. You were living in an apartment. You were only there for a week or so, and then you decided it was too expensive. A friend of mine was looking for somewhere to rent, and he took over your lease. The day you moved out I came to visit him. And that's where we met—at that apartment in Vienna.'

'Of course,' cried Kitty. 'Yes, of course—I remember now. That's quite right, we have met before. How is your friend, by the way? And how long have you been here?'

'I've only just arrived.'

Immediately there was a bond between them. Alec was a divorcee with a sixteen-year-old daughter named Vera. After some months of this growing friendship Alec asked Kitty to marry him. Well, thought Kitty, he already has a daughter, so if I really can't have any children, if the specialist was right, then it won't matter so much.

She said 'yes', and at Christmas time, in 1953, Kitty Kalafoni and Alec Diosy were married.

Shortly after her wedding Kitty began looking around for a better job. Alec was a draftsman at the gas company, and he spoke to a client of his, Reg Kelly, at Liddle and Epstein Air Conditioning (a subsidiary of Honeywell). Kitty was interviewed and offered a position in their accounts department—where she was to stay for many years.

Slowly her new life was putting layers of forgetfulness over Kitty's bitter memories.

Some time later, much to her delight and astonishment, Kitty became pregnant. But the delight ended in grief, when the pregnancy ended in a miscarriage.

Twice more she became pregnant, and twice more miscarried. After the second miscarriage, Dr Loxton, a specialist gynaecologist, advised Kitty that further pregnancies would be dangerous for her, and that she should have a hysterectomy. Distressed by this advice she returned to her GP who advised her to see a Dr O'Shea, an obstetrician at St Margaret's Hospital.

Becoming pregnant for a fourth time, Kitty went to see him, and told him what the gynaecologists had told her—first in Vienna, and then in Sydney.

'Well,' replied Dr O'Shea, 'let's see if we can prove them wrong. Do you want to have this child?'

'I'm 39 years of age. This is my last chance. I really want to have this baby.'

'And since you are pregnant we will do everything we can to help you carry this baby to full term.'

Each month Kitty saw him for a check up, and for a series of injections. Dr O'Shea insisted that she rest as much as possible, and he fussed over her, and took great care of her throughout that pregnancy (and made it possible for Kitty to keep working at Liddle and Epstein throughout that time).

On September 1, 1959, Kitty's daughter Juliette was born.

32

KITTY HAD A CAREER, a husband, a home and a daughter. She should have been happy. Indeed, often she was—very happy.

But there was still an unresolved bitterness in her heart. There were times when she lay on her bed, unable to sleep, remembering the executed bodies of Nazi collaborators that had been hung from lampposts in the centre of Budapest. And that memory, at least, pleased her. But then she remembered all the unforgivable things that had been done to her, to her father, to her family, to Hédi...to so many people. Sometimes she remembered the face of Adolf Hitler, seen from just a few feet away, at a moment when he was glowing with triumphant cunning—and was about to inflict measureless pain on millions—and she would feel a flash of burning anger.

In 1972 a course of events began that was to remove that bitterness, and that dark shadow, from Kitty's life forever.

At the age of 13, her daughter Juliette started high school. She had attended Rose Bay Primary School, and then an Opportunity Class for gifted children, and had won a scholarship to Kambala School for Girls, a distinguished private school, run by the Anglican Church.

Meanwhile, the relationship between Kitty and her husband Alec had deteriorated badly. They had discovered they were very different people, communicating on different wavelengths, and disagreeing about almost everything. Juliette remembers them arguing often in those years, and remembers Kitty as a typical 'hot-headed Hungarian.' Kitty remembers this as a time of frustration, when Alec would retreat behind his newspaper rather than discuss the issues between them.

And, of course, they disagreed about which school Juliette should attend.

Back in Hungary, decades before, Alec's grandfather (at the time a colonel in the Hungarian army) had converted from Judaism to Roman Catholicism to advance his military career. Hence, Alec had been born into a Roman Catholic family, and been sent to the leading private Roman Catholic school in Budapest. He had even visited Rome, with a group from his class, as a 16-year-old schoolboy. But as an adult he had turned angrily against all faiths of all kinds. Despite his enthusiasm for the best education for Juliette, he was not keen on sending his daughter to a church School. It was Kitty who pushed for a 'good private school' for Juliette, and entered their daughter for the scholarship exams.

Following her birth at St Margaret's Hospital, Juliette had been baptized. Since Kitty had a certificate, acquired by her and her parents in Budapest, showing her to be Roman Catholic, not Jewish, she regarded herself as being "officially" Roman Catholic. So, shortly after Juliette's birth, Kitty, who was overjoyed about the arrival of the baby she had been warned she could never have, told a Roman Catholic priest at the hospital she wanted her daughter baptized.

'Where do you go to church?' he asked.

'Well ...we don't actually go to church at all,' Kitty confessed.

'I see. In which church were you married, then?'

'To tell the truth...we were married in the registry office.'

It quickly became apparent that he could see little point in the child being baptized as a Roman Catholic.

As he was leaving the ward, the priest stopped, turned around and said, 'Go to your Hungarian priest.'

Nothing could have been more offensive to Kitty. Living in Australia she was determined to be as Australian as possible, and had little patience with those members of the Hungarian community who wanted to be more Hungarian than Australian. Kitty had already decided never to talk to her daughter in Hungarian—only ever in English.

'Very well,' thought Kitty to herself, 'if not Roman Catholic, then Church of England.'

Having her daughter baptized as an Anglican fitted well with her determination to be thoroughly integrated into her new country. 'I am Australian now,' Kitty would explain, 'and our daughter is Australian, and I want her to be as Australian as it is possible to be. Most Australians seem to be Anglican, so that is the religion that Juliette should have.'

In part at least, this was one reason why Kitty was happy with the idea of Juliette attending an Anglican private school—even though she herself never attended church, and Alec insisted he'd have to be dead before he entered a church. 'And preferably,' he added, 'not even then.'

Juliette was not sent to church or Sunday school as a child, and, although she says she had a strong sense of God—the idea of a creator just seemed logical to her—she knew nothing about what Christians believe, and nothing about Jesus and the Bible.

At her new school Juliette fell in with a group of girls and became particular friends with Kate Fitzpatrick. At the time Kate was a boarder and so was required to go to church on Sundays. For Juliette and Kate to spend any time together on the weekends was almost impossible, so Juliette started going to church and Sunday school with Kate each Sunday morning.

Juliette was surprised that Kitty and Alec allowed her to go. 'Perhaps,' she says, 'they were just happy that I had found a friend.' Her closeness to Kate was increased by the hostility she felt coming from her Jewish classmates. 'How can you call yourself Church of England?' they used to demand of Juliette. 'Your mother is a Jew. That makes you a Jew. You can't be anything but a Jew. You're a Jew just like us.'

The Sunday school, the church services, and later the youth group at St Michael's were the places where Juliette learned for the first time what Christians really believe about Jesus and the Bible—and where she eventually became a real Christian.

She still remembers one Sunday morning in 1973 when their Sunday School teacher Simon Manchester explained to the class that the Christian faith was not some sort of heavenly insurance policy. 'Don't imagine,' he said, 'that on your deathbed you will suddenly turn to God and ask for forgiveness and acceptance. If you have ignored God all your life there's no reason to assume that you won't still ignore God even on your death bed.'

'But do we really need to be forgiven?' asked young Juliette.

'If you think you don't need forgiveness,' Simon explained with a smile, 'try to do nothing wrong for just 24 hours. For one day try to do, and say, and think, absolutely nothing wrong—not even slightly wrong.'

Juliette took up the challenge. So for 24 hours she tried not to do or think or say anything that would offend God, or his high standards, and would not offend, or annoy or hurt or bother the people around her. She quickly realised that it was impossible, and that she needed to accept God's offer of forgiveness. From this realization came her personal commitment to the Christian faith.

And there were events that strongly confirmed Juliette in the step she had taken. One was the funeral of a young man named Peter Hobart, who died from cancer at the age of 26. The church was packed, but what impressed her was the atmosphere, the spirit, of the occasion. 'What stands out in my mind,' she said later, 'was the amazing sense of thanksgiving for his life. There was a completely positive sense of knowing where he was, and that he had passed from suffering to paradise.' Earlier, she had had a similar experience when Jonathan Manchester—the brother of Simon and her friend Jane—had died at the age of

17, from a drowning accident in his backyard swimming pool. His funeral too was a positive celebration of a young life, and an expression of certainty about his eternal destiny.

Juliette had more discussions with her father than her mother about her new-found faith. Although Alec was unsympathetic towards her beliefs he was happy that she was mixing with a nice group of people, and thought it protection against getting into trouble or mixing with undesirable boys. Perhaps for these reasons Juliette remembers no animosity from Alec to her faith.

33

EARLY IN THE FIRST school term in 1973 the parents of Kambala girls were invited to attend the first Parent and Teacher night of the year.

Alec was not interested in attending. 'I don't want to meet the parents of those Kambala kids,' he growled to his wife. 'You go.'

So Kitty went.

As soon as she entered the large room she knew that Alec would have hated being there. Many of those present were members of the local Hungarian community—the women in diamonds and furs, and, to Kitty's disgust, speaking loudly to each other in Hungarian.

'Why can't they just accept that this is not Hungary?' thought Kitty to herself as she took her place in a long queue to speak to a teacher. 'Why can't they be happy just to be Australian?'

'We're just going to have to be patient, I think,' said the lady in front of Kitty in the queue, interrupting these thoughts.

'I'm sorry, my mind was elsewhere,' Kitty apologised.

'It's just that the queue is moving very slowly,' explained the woman, who had a pleasant, friendly face and the warmest smile Kitty had ever seen. It was that smile, Kitty was to say later, that captivated her immediately.

'Ah, well, there are some nice people in the room,' thought Kitty as she nodded in agreement.

'Still, we all want to spend as long as possible with the teacher talking about our daughters, I suppose,' the woman continued, 'so we can't blame people for that.'

As their conversation continued Kitty felt immediately at home with this woman, as comfortable as if she had known her for a long time.

At that moment Kate's mother, Margaret Fitzpatrick, walked up to where they were standing in the queue.

'Ah,' said Margaret with a smile, 'I see that you've met Gloria.'

'We've only just met,' Kitty said. 'We haven't even introduced ourselves yet.'

'This is Gloria Short,' said Margaret with a smile, making the introductions, 'Ken Short's wife—you know the minister of St Michael's.'

'Oh, yes, of course—Marion's mother.'

'So, you are Juliette's mother!' said Gloria, with a delighted smile of recognition. She knew Juliette through the church.

'Why,' continued Gloria, 'haven't I seen you at church? Juliette comes to church, to youth group and Sunday School.'

Margaret was later to remember that Kitty, who was wrapped up against the cold, looked quite dejected and unhappy that night. And Gloria was later to remember that she had first spoken to Kitty because she looked so lost and alone.

'Now why,' repeated Gloria, 'haven't I seen you at church?'

Grasping for an excuse, Kitty remembered her piece of paper

and her official classification, and said, 'I'm a Roman Catholic.'

'Oh, that doesn't matter. You can still come to our church. In fact, I wish you would. You'd be more than welcome. I could watch out for you, wait for you at the door.'

That night Kitty lay awake in bed long after Alec had fallen asleep, thinking, 'Now what shall I do? What have I let myself in for? I don't know anything about the Anglican church. I don't know anything about any church. I don't know anything about God, even. What do I do now? She was such a nice lady, that Gloria, I really liked her. How can I let her down by not turning up at her church?'

Kitty lay in the dark remembering things that Juliette had said about the Shorts—about what a wonderful family they were, and what nice people Marion and her sister Kathy and brother David were, and their parents, Ken and Gloria. If Juliette was so impressed with them there must be something there, but how, Kitty wondered, could I get involved? How could a Hungarian refugee, a "displaced person", from a non-religious Jewish family, with a piece of paper identifying her as a Roman Catholic, who believed nothing and knew nothing, be a part of such a group of people?

The question that exercised Kitty's mind was, 'How can I, as a mother, better support Juliette? How can I give Juliette what Gloria and Margaret are giving their children?' Kitty did not deceive herself, and she knew that as much as she loved her parents they had been godless, self-centred and self-indulgent. So she kept asking herself how she could give Juliette what she herself had missed out on.

Throughout the next day, whenever there was a pause in the busy rhythm of her work, Kitty would begin to think, 'There is something extra that I want to give Juliette. Something extra I can see in Gloria and Margaret. But how can I give her something I've never had myself?'

That afternoon, when she arrived back in their apartment after a day at the office, she found a visiting card lying on the carpet—having been slipped under the front door. On the card were the words: *Rev Ken Short, Rector, St Michael's, Vaucluse*, followed by the phone number.

On the back was a scribbled note, *'Please call and let me know when you'll be home. I'd like to pop around for a visit.'*

'That's what religious people do,' was Alec's comment. 'They try to get their claws into you. You're not going to ring him, are you? You're not going to invite him around?'

'I don't know what I'll do,' Kitty said. 'I've never talked to a minister in my life. What could I possibly talk to him about? A pot of tea and an embarrassed silence—that's what a visit would be. But I can't ignore him—he knows Juliette. What do I do now?'

'Do nothing,' Alec advised. 'You can ignore him. Put your mind to it—you can do it. Ignore the card, pretend he never called.'

For the next two days Kitty was thinking about what to do, and then she came home to find another card slipped under the front door of the apartment.

'I have no excuse,' Kitty muttered ruefully, as she picked up the second visiting card, 'I'll have to ring now.'

She made herself a cup of coffee, and then sat down and dialled the number.

When Ken answered the phone she introduced herself and apologised, 'I'm sorry I didn't ring earlier, and I'm sorry you keep missing me—but I'm at work every day.'

'That doesn't matter,' responded the cheerful voice on the telephone. 'What are you doing on Saturday?'

'The washing.'

'Well, put off the washing for an hour, and I'll be there at ten o'clock.'

When Alec heard about the appointment he announced that

he would be going out on Saturday morning.

'I don't want to meet any ministers. I'll be going out early, and I'll be back late. I'm taking no risk of running into that man.'

Ken arrived promptly at ten o'clock the following Saturday morning. Kitty found him to be as warm and friendly as his wife Gloria. She made tea, and then they sat down in the lounge to talk. And they talked for the next two and a half hours.

The conversation began with general chat about the weather, about Juliette, about many things. But he was such an easy man to talk to, that before long Kitty found herself saying, 'I'm not a believer. I'm nothing really. I was born Jewish, but our family was not at all religious. We only ever went to synagogue once a year, and didn't celebrate any of the special days, or bother much about kosher food.'

'Non-observing Jews?'

'Yes, that's right. And then, at the start of the war my father decided that we all had to become Roman Catholics to protect us from the Nazi threat. It didn't work, but we weren't to know that in advance, and so we did it.'

'And did you understand what that meant?'

'All I ever understood was that you couldn't really go to communion, to Mass, unless you confessed to a priest first. And I just never felt I could do that. I didn't want to do that.'

'There are no barriers. There are no formulas and no rituals. God welcomes everybody who really wants to come to him. What God offers everyone who will come is his friendship, his forgiveness and a place in his family.'

'Oh? That's different from what I had understood.'

In the long conversation that followed Kitty found herself explaining that she had never ceased to believe that God was actually there, somewhere. Even in the darkest days, and when the most horrible things happened, it was still just obvious to her, common sense really, that a world as complex as this must have Someone behind it.

And she never blamed God for the horrors of anti-Semitism. She blamed people for that. She still blamed the Nazis and the *Nyilas* for that. When she stopped to think about it, she was still angry about what they had done. She had no forgiveness in her heart for them. But she didn't blame God.

As far as Kitty was concerned God was simply very remote. So far off as not to be worth even thinking about. Unapproachable, and, most probably, not interested in us if we did approach him.

Ken explained that the gap Kitty was aware of—the gap between us and God—is very real. But also that the gap has been bridged—from God's side.

'That's who Jesus is,' said Ken. 'The bridge back to God. Jesus died to pay for all the horror, and all the evil, the very small wrong things in all our lives, as well as the big horrors, so that we can return to God and be welcomed home. And Jesus came back from the dead to take us personally across that bridge. Jesus opens the door, welcomes us home, and makes us part of God's family—which is where we are meant to be, where we belong. The only door back to God is marked "Forgiveness"—and Jesus is that door. He is the one who can forgive us. If we want him to. If we ask him to.'

'I had no idea that Jesus did that, or that Jesus was so impor-tant—no idea at all. At one stage in my life I did go to church, but I know nothing about Jesus.'

In the early years of the war, Kitty explained, when life was still relatively normal in Budapest, she used to go, every Sunday, to St Stephen's Basilica—because it was within walking distance of Academia Street, and because her godmother, Irma Benes, wanted her to attend church.

'It was a beautiful building,' she said. 'As beautiful as an opera house. And the music was solemn and magnificent. Near one of the doors there was a statue of St Anthony, and every time I walked past I used to touch the big toe of the statue—for luck.'

'Why did you go?'

'Irma was a nice woman, and she wanted me to go. She was a God-fearing lady. She took flowers to church each week. And, anyway, it was only four blocks from our apartment in Academia Street, just a short walk. And I suppose I thought God would be pleased with me if I went to church. I might feel a bit closer to God, and I might understand a bit more.'

'And did you understand?'

'No. In those days it was all in Latin, and I could understand none of it. I certainly heard nothing about Jesus, and knew nothing about Jesus.'

'Well, did it make you feel any closer to God?'

'No. It was just a...it's hard to explain...just a mystical thing. It was nice. The building was magnificent and the music was lovely. But God remained as remote as ever. My ideas about God are very vague.'

'The place where God speaks to us,' Ken explained, 'is in the Bible. That's where we can learn about Jesus and hear his voice. Have you ever read the Bible?'

'I tried to once. In 1956 when I became a naturalised citizen of Australia I was presented with a small Bible. I tried to read it, but it was in old English, and I didn't know where to start, and I didn't understand what I was reading, so I gave up very quickly. Also, I suppose, in those days, my English wasn't all that good.'

As their conversation went on Kitty found herself explaining to Ken how she felt that she didn't belong. She didn't belong to Hungary any longer, and she only belonged to Australia as a late-arrival, not a native; she didn't belong to the Jews; she didn't belong to the Roman Catholics—she didn't belong anywhere. That was how she felt. Although her mother was still alive, her father and all her male relatives had been killed in the death camps. If she had gone back to Budapest she would have found not one single living relative there. She felt as though she deserved the label they had once given her: "displaced person."

'You are God's child,' replied Ken, 'and he sent his one and only Son, Jesus, into this world to rescue you—to reclaim you, to forgive you, and to change you. What you need to do is trust the God who loves you like that.'

Somehow the word 'forgiveness' kept coming up in his conversation. And somehow Kitty understood that she needed to understand what he was saying and how it applied to her. The next day she went to church. Gloria Short had kept her word, and was at the front door watching out for her.

She introduced Kitty to some others who were members of the church "family." Some of them, became close friends, whose friendship would last for many years. Gloria took her inside the church, and Kitty was surprised to discover that the large building was full—every pew was packed.

The following Wednesday night Kitty went to a Bible study group led by Ken and continued to attend that weekly Bible study group for the next few years.

On those Wednesday nights Ken's practice was to teach the group from carefully researched and prepared notes on the Bible passage they were studying. He would speak for 40 to 50 minutes. 'But every so often,' he says, 'I would pause to draw breath and that's when the questions would come from Kitty. And in her questions there was often a sense of her dark, difficult personal history, a sense of the past that she was wrestling with. Her "what if..." questions hinted at the horrors she had seen, and the terrible experiences she had endured. There was clearly a lot of unresolved anger and bitterness there at first. She was clearly re-living these things, and allowing the Bible to speak to them. She seemed to move forward just a little each Wednesday night, not a lot. It was a gradual process.'

To Kitty it was all so new that she was like a sponge, just soaking up all this information from the Bible. Slowly, over time, the shadow hanging over Kitty's heart began to dissipate. The hard lump of bitterness deep within began to dissolve.

The following year, 1974, Kitty's birthday, June 16th, fell on a Sunday. That particular Sunday Ken preached a sermon in which he made it clear that knowing about Jesus and the Bible was not enough. This was, he said, a message that required a response. It was more than mere information—it was an invitation from the Living God. It required a response of the heart and mind: a deliberate, conscious, knowing response of commitment. That day Kitty responded. She asked Jesus to forgive her, and change her, and take over the running of her life both now and forever.

'This is what I really want,' she was able to say, 'both for myself and for my daughter.'

The response from her husband was not encouraging.

'All my life I've been looking for something,' Kitty tried to explain. 'I didn't know what it was, I didn't know what I wanted, but I was looking for something—something more than angry memories...Now I've found it. That's the only way I can explain it. There is a Someone, a Person, who is supposed to be in charge of my life, and of everyone's life. Well, I've asked him to take over. Jesus is in charge now. Oh, I know I'm not perfect, a long way from it—*but I am forgiven*. Until now my life has been empty, artificial. I've been looking for something really solid. Until now I've had no foundation for my life. But now I have experienced forgiveness, and...well...the only way to explain it is to say that my heart has been changed...I am able to forgive everything that has ever happened to me. That shadow of anger and bitterness has finally gone. Seeing Jesus, asking him to take over running my life, has finally driven away the shadow of Hitler, and all the evil, and pain and suffering he caused.'

Alec buried his head in the newspaper as Kitty continued, 'Now I've found the foundation, the Person I belong to, and I've found...my life.'

34

THE YEARS THAT FOLLOWED brought their difficulties as well as their joys.

As the relationship between Kitty and Alec became ever more difficult it was eventually clear that a separation was inevitable. They chose not to divorce, but simply to live apart. Kitty and Juliette set up in a new apartment but maintained regular contact with Alec.

Juliette remembers this as a dark time: 'This was such a black period of my life for me. I remember being given a choice of who I wanted to live with: Mum or Dad. I chose to live with Mum because I was certain that with her I could keep going to church.'

Juliette also remembers having a number of talks with Alec about his need to find peace with God. 'His biggest problem,' says Juliette, 'was that he didn't think he was all that bad—didn't think that he needed forgiveness, that God should look at his life, give him five out of ten, and accept him. He couldn't accept that he needed forgiveness just as much as some murderer in the newspaper—as much as every single one of us does. But perhaps he came to terms with God before he died. I certainly hope he did.'

Juliette moved on from Kambala to university, and to life as a wife and mother. And in due course Kitty, who had once been warned that she could never be a mother, became a grandmother.

And Kitty's inner journey came to rest in a safe haven. In finding peace with God, Kitty found a deep inner peace that cast its light back over the whole of her life, and enabled her to think about her wartime experiences without anger and without bitterness.

She tried to explain to her mother about the great change that had come into her life. But to Ada the things that Kitty said were simply incomprehensible.

Ada had remarried years before (to an Austrian-born Sydney tobacconist named Norbert Salzman) and lived not far from Kitty at Elizabeth Bay. Although Ada remained a non-practising Jew all her life she angrily told Kitty that becoming a Christian made her 'a traitor... worse than a traitor—an anti-semite.'

'But Mama, I have learned how to forgive,' Kitty replied. 'Now that I have experienced God's forgiveness and God's peace, I am able to forgive those people who did such appalling things—to me, to Papa, and you, and all of our family. I have forgiven all the hurt that was inflicted, and now I have no bitterness. I know that when I go back to Hungary there is nobody there—not a single close relative—but somehow God has dealt with that anger and bitterness that I once harboured in my heart. I can look back on those years, and I can even talk about what happened then, and I feel no anger any more. That anger has all gone. It is being forgiven myself—by God, through Jesus—that enables me to forgive.'

Ada's life in Sydney was comfortable. She never needed to work, and she and her husband had frequent holidays in Europe. But as far as she was concerned no comforts, no luxuries, could ever balance what the holocaust had taken away.

'Unforgivable,' muttered Ada angrily. 'What those Nazi thugs did was unforgivable. And if you think you can forgive them, and put those memories behind you, then you've gone soft in the head. I shall never forgive, and never forget. I shall maintain my anger until the day I die.'

No words of Kitty's could ever reach her mother on this topic. And when Ada died in 1989 she was still nursing bitterness and hatred against the Nazis who had destroyed her comfortable life in pre-war Budapest. She went to her grave with her anger still burning.

In January 2001, Kitty attended an annual Summer School run by the Church Missionary Society (CMS). She went with her friend Betty Powell—Betty's husband Ken having died the previous year. As she struggled through the gate of the conference centre with her bag, Kitty heard a woman's voice saying, 'Here, let me help you with that.'

'No, no I can manage,' Kitty replied, but the younger woman insisted. Kitty noticed that the she had a thick European accent.

'Where are you from?'

'Germany, originally.'

The young woman introduced herself as Hanna Collison. Hanna and her husband Max (with their three children Tim, Katrin and John) were CMS missionaries in Kenya.

'We must have a proper talk together,' said Kitty, 'a real talk—before Summer School is over.' Hanna readily agreed.

Max and Hanna worked in the slums of Nairobi. Max had established a network of self-supporting clinics where even the poorest slum dwellers could receive medical treatment. By using Christian volunteers costs were kept to a minimum.

Over the next few days Kitty came to know the Collisons well, as they too were staying at the CMS Centre.

That last night they sat in the dining room and began to talk about themselves and their backgrounds.

'I was born in Budapest,' said Kitty. 'What about you?'

'Essen—in western Germany,' Hanna replied, 'that's where I was born and grew up.'

Kitty went on to explain about growing up Jewish in Hungary, about losing every male member of her family in the death camps during World War Two, and about some of the horrors she, herself, had experienced. As she did so Hanna froze.

Hanna felt that sudden hollow feeling in the pit of the stomach that comes when something has to be confronted that has been avoided for a long time.

The history of the Second World War and the holocaust haunted Hanna, even though it had all happened before she was born. Her father had been a soldier in Hitler's SS—compelled to join when he turned 18. He had been a foot soldier during the advance into Poland in 1939. In January 1941 he was seriously wounded, and took no further active part in the war.

As Hanna had learned the history of those years she had always assumed that her father had—personally—never done anything wrong. He was a gentle, softly spoken man—and he was Hanna's beloved father—and she believed him incapable of the atrocities she heard and read about. He never talked about the war. He had been very young, had been invalided out of the SS early in the conflict, and the memories of that time were, clearly, too painful for him to discuss.

But even if there was no direct guilt in her family Hanna was intensely aware of what her country had done, and what misery her nation had inflicted on so many. Essen, where she grew up, was a major industrial city where many of the armaments and weapons were manufactured for Hitler during the Second World War.

Now, she was facing a woman who had suffered at German hands in World War Two.

This was the first time Hanna had ever met a Jewish man or woman of that war generation face to face. Could any Jewish person ever forgive a German for what had happened? All of this was running rapidly through Hanna's mind as Kitty spoke.

She felt the colour drain out of her face.

When Kitty had finished speaking Hanna said quietly, 'Then

you must not like me. I'm sure you must hate me. I am German by birth. It was my country that did all of those things to your family.'

'Not at all!' Kitty cried. 'You are my sister in Christ and I love you. When I became a Christian I forgave everything that had ever happened to me or my family. You mustn't feel that way. We are together, we are sisters, there is no barrier between us.'

Both women had tears in their eyes. A moment later they were hugging and weeping. Hanna felt that Kitty's words were a gift from God—liberating her from a lifetime of guilt and concern over the suffering her country, her people, had inflicted. She had long known about God's gracious and generous forgiveness—but now she *felt* forgiven. She wanted to shout it out. She wanted to hurry back to Kenya to share the experience with a fellow missionary, a woman from the former East Germany, who carried the same burden.

Kitty and Hanna were no longer German and Jew—they were one in Jesus Christ.

Kitty had found the place where the human heart finds rest. She had found forgiveness. And in that forgiveness she had found a rich treasure she could share.

Kathy Diosy 2003

If I were God...
I'd End all the pain

A child catches a rare brain virus and is affected for life. A father dies in a plane crash. A dictator murders millions. Why doesn't God do something about things like this? Can we still believe in God in the face of all the suffering and pain in the world? John Dickson looks honestly at these questions and provides some compelling answers. He looks briefly at the alternative explanations offered by the world's religions before turning to what the Bible itself says about God, justice and suffering.

Simply Christianity:

Beyond Religion

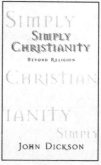

One of the reasons people sometimes avoid looking into Christianity is that there are so many versions on offer, each with its own religious package. The project of this book is to get beyond the rituals, myth and dogma.

By going back to the earliest biographies of Jesus—the Gospels in the New Testament—*Simply Christianity* finds what remains after the 'religion' is stripped away. It's a great book for understanding the core of Christian faith.

Order From:

The Good Book Company
Telephone: 0845-225-0880
Facsimile: 0845-225-0990
Email: admin@thegoodbook.co.uk
Website: www.thegoodbook.co.uk